WEIGHT WATCHERS FREESTYLE 2020

New Year And New Weight Watchers Freestyle Recipes For A New YOU!

By J Beckam

© Copyright 2019 by J Beckam All rights reserved.

The following Book is reproduced below with the goal of providing information that is as accurate and as reliable as possible. Regardless, purchasing this eBook can be seen as consent to the fact that both the publisher and the author of this book are in no way experts on the topics discussed within, and that any recommendations or suggestions made herein are for entertainment purposes only. Professionals should be consulted as needed before undertaking any of the action endorsed herein.

This declaration is deemed fair and valid by both the American Bar Association and the Committee of Publishers Association and is legally binding throughout the United States.

Furthermore, the transmission, duplication or reproduction of any of the following work, including precise information, will be considered an illegal act, irrespective whether it is done electronically or in print. The legality extends to creating a secondary or tertiary copy of the work or a recorded copy and is only allowed with express written consent of the Publisher. All additional rights are reserved.

The information in the following pages is broadly considered a truthful and accurate account of facts, and as such, any inattention, use or misuse of the information in question by the reader will render any resulting actions solely under their purview. There are no scenarios in which the publisher or the original author of this work can be in any fashion deemed liable for any hardship or damages that may befall them after undertaking information described herein.
Additionally, the information found on the following pages is intended for informational purposes only and should thus be considered, universal. As befitting its nature, the information presented is without assurance regarding its continued validity or interim quality. Trademarks that mentioned are done without written consent and can in no way be considered an endorsement from the trademark holder.

TABLE OF CONTENTS

Introduction 8
   the New Freesyle Program: 9
My Favorite Freestyle Recipes 16
   0FS Points – GreekStyle Chickpea Salad 17
   0FS Points - Grilled Shrimp Marinade 18
   0FS Points - Vegetarian Chili in Instant Pot 19
   0FS Points - Mexican Chicken Soup 20
   0FS Points - Zero Points Bean Soup: 21
   1FS Points - Chicken Taco Soup Recipe 21
   1FS Points - Sweet & Sour Turkey Meatballs 22
   2FS Points - Tasty BBQ Apricot Chicken 22
   2FS Points - Grilled Cream Corn 23
   2FS Points - Greek Yogurt Egg Omelet 23
   2FS Points - Mashed Sweet Potatoes 24
   3FS Points - Savory Chicken Dump Soup 24
   4FS points - Bruschetta Topped Balsamic Chicken 25
   4FS Points - Vegan Stuffing Soup 27
   4FS Points - African Sweet Potato Stew 27
   5FS Points - Creamy-Tomato-Basil-Soup 28
   5FS Points - Roasted Sweet Potato Side Dish 29
   0FS Points - Greek Chickpea Salad 29
   0FS Points - Crock Pot Chicken Cacciatore 31
   0FS Points - Succotash Bean Soup 31
   0FS Points - Slow Cook Chicken Cacciatore 32
   5FS Points - Chicken Marsala MeatBall 32
   5FS Points - Tasty Turkey Meatball & Veggie 34
   5FS Points - Garlic Roasted Garbanzo Beans 35
   5FS Points - Sticky Buffalo Chicken Tenders 35
   5FS Points - Ham & Apricot Dijon Glaze 36
   6FS Points - Pimento South American Chicken 36
   7FS Points - Pizza Lasagna Roll-Ups 37
   7FS points - Apple Cheddar Turkey Wraps 38
Breakfasts Recipes 40
   2PTS So Tasty Meat Soufflé 41
   3PTS Breakfast Tasty Quiche 42
   3PTS Delicious Mexican Breakfast 43
   1PTS Simple Breakfast Pancakes 44
   4PTS Egg, Bacon, and Hash Browns 45

- 4PTS Oatmeal Muffin with Applesauce 46
- 4PTS Avocado and Pear Smoothie 47
- 5PTS Muffins with Lemon Poppy Seeds 48
- 6PTS Tasty Hash Browns Omelet 49
- 5PTS Wholesome Strawberry Bruschetta 50
- 4PTS Raisin Bread with Pineapple 51
- 5PTS Energizing Breakfast Burrito 52
- 2PTS Coconut and Raspberry Smoothie 53
- 4PTS Quick Buckwheat Porridge 54
- 4PTS Healthy Squash Porridge 55
- 4PTS Instant Orange Smoothie 56
- 5PTS Fruit, Vegetable and Herb Smoothie 57
- 3PTS Peaches and Cream Oatmeal Delight 58
- 5PTS Apple and Cranberry Oatmeal 59
- 3PTS Creamy Banana French Toast 60
- 4PTS Low Carb Breakfast Porridge 61
- 5PTS Dairy-Free Pear Oatmeal 62

Chicken Recipes 63

- 6PTS Chicken Okra Soup 64
- 12PTS Vinegar Chicken 65
- 9PTS Chicken Cola Wings 66
- 6PTS Honey Sesame Chicken 67
- 3PTS Tasty Orange Chicken 68
- 5PTS Cajun Chicken and Sweet Potato Hash 69
- 5PTS Instant Fajita Casserole 70
- 3PTS Baked Artichoke Chicken 71
- 6PTS Garlic Thai Chicken 72
- 3PTS Creamy Dijon Chicken 73
- 4PTS Light Chicken Salad 74
- 8PTS Chili Turkey Macaroni with Jalapenos 75
- 6PTS Grilled Chicken Salad 76
- 4PTS Tasty Chicken Fried Rice 77
- 4PTS Pressure Cook Chicken Salad 78
- 5PTS Raspberry Balsamic Chicken 79
- 7PTS Instant Pot Vegetable Duck 80

Pork, Veal and Lamb 81

- 5PTS Spiced Pork with Apples 82
- 4PTS Pork Chops with Salsa 83
- 7PTS Balsamic Pork Tenderloin with Roasted Broccoli Rabe 84

- 5PTS Real Easy Pork Piccata 85
- 5PTS Slow Cooker Spiced Pulled Pork 86
- 9PTS Healthy Curried Pork Chops 87
- 8PTS Spicy Pineapple Pork 88
- 6PTS Breaded Veal Cutlets 89
- 5PTS Pecan Lemony Veal Cutlets 90
- 7PTS Lamb Skewers with Cool Mint Sauce 91
- 6PTS Garlic Infused Roasted Leg of Lamb 92

Beef Rcipes 93
- 8PTS Slow Cooked Full of Flavor Beef Chili 94
- 8PTS Skillet Teriyaki Beef 95
- 7PTS Beef with Herbs Recipe 96
- 6PTS Beef Breast Pieces with Celery 97
- 8PTS Beef with Potato Instant Pot Recipe 98
- 6PTS Beef Steak with Tomato Soup 99
- 5PTS Beef with Mushrooms Pot Recipe 100
- 6PTS Simple Beef Recipe 101
- 9PTS Grilled Steak and Sweet Potatoes Skewers 102
- 7PTS Eastern Island Beef Stew 103
- 6PTS Ground Beef with Spinach Leaves 104
- 6PTS Beef with Beans Recipe 105
- 8PTS Beef Steak with Mustard 106
- 7PTS Beef Worcestershire Recipe 107
- 8PTS Maple Syrup Mix Beef Recipe 108
- 5PTS Creole Crusted Ribeye's 109
- 5PTS Beef Medallions with Rosemary Mushroom Sauce 110
- 5PTS Authentic Italian Steak Rolls 111
- 8PTS Instant Beef Soba Bowls 112
- 5PTS Tradition Beef Rope Viejas 113
- 7PTS Steak with Leek Pan Sauce 114
- 6PTS Cool and Tangy Beef Cups 115

Fish and Seafood Recipes 116
- 2PTS Ponzu Pockets 117
- 1PTS Lemon Dijon Whitefish 118
- 3PTS Creamy Cucumber Salmon 119
- 4PTS Salmon Glazed with Honey 120
- 3PTS Real Easy Glazed Salmon 121
- 8PTS Angel Hair Shrimp and Tomato Pasta 122
- 5PTS Simple Pasta and Tuna Salad 123

- 5PTS Salmon in Ginger and Soy 124
- 7PTS Grilled Shrimp and Watermelon Salad 125
- 7PTS Low Points Shrimp with Pasta 126
- 8PTS Tasty Baked Curry Scallops 127
- 3PTS Baked Shrimp with Spices 128
- 4PTS Simple Coastal Tuna Salad 129

Salads and Soups 130
- 6PTS Raspberry Chicken Salad 131
- 5PTS Asparagus and Stilton Chicken Salad 131
- 4PTS Chicken and Spinach Crescent Rings 132
- 5PTS Tender Chicken Club Salad 132
- 6PTS Roasted Caprese Salad with Chicken 133
- 4PTS Pumpkin Taste Soup Recipe 134
- 6PTS Turkey Mixed Soup Recipe 135
- 3PTS Mushrooms Soup Recipe 136
- 4PTS Simple Chicken and Green Onion Soup 137
- 5PTS Instant Pot Egg Salad 137
- 4PTS Spinach, Pears and Blue Cheese Tossed Salad 138
- 8PTS Delicious Sweet Potato Chili 138
- 6PTS Roasted Cauliflower and Fennel Soup 139
- 5PTS Quick French Onion Soup 140
- 5PTS Oyster Mushroom Egg Drop Soup 140
- 3PTS Chicken and Egg Soup 141

Vegetarian Recipes 142
- 4PTS Zucchini Soba Noodles 143
- 5PTS Perfect Garden Pasta 144
- 7PTS Chickpea and Spinach Frittata 145
- 7PTS Mediterranean Stuffed Sweet Potatoes 146
- 8PTS Eggplant and Couscous Ragu 147
- 5PTS Vegetarian Pita Pizza 148
- 3PTS Corn Tomato Salad 149
- 5PTS Cauliflower and Black Beans 150
- 5PTS Zucchini Cashew Noodles 151

Side Dishes and Snacks 152
- 2PTS Sesame Asparagus 153
- 2PTS Herbed Green Beans 154
- 3PTS Fresh Spinach Muffins 155
- 3PTS Crisp Fennel and Pear 156
- 3PTS Shaved Brussels sprouts with Walnuts 157

2PTS Creamy Carrot Slaw 158

3PTS Decadent Mushrooms 159

5PTS Lemon Walnut Quinoa 160

2PTS Spiced Brussels sprouts 161

Desserts Recipes 162

2PTS Tasty Cupcake Brownies 163

5PTS Quick Banana Roll Ups 164

4PTS Fruit and Pudding Mix Dessert 165

1PTS Banana "Ice Cream" Dessert 166

0PTS No Point Banana Strawberry "Ice Cream" Dessert 167

1PTS Simple Frozen Fruit Dessert..168

2PTS Coconut and Cranberry Macaroons 169

2PTS Frozen Peanut Butter Cups 170

2PTS Instant Pot Truffles 171

3PTS Yummy Pumpkin Pudding 172

End Note 172

INTRODUCTION

The reasons why people lose weight vary from person to person. Over the past two decades, obesity has greatly increased in the USA with statistics showing that more than a third of adults in the USA are overweight. When one is overweight, he or she has a lot of physiological as well as emotional issues, hence people having varied reasons for wanting to lose weight:

THE NEW FREESYLE PROGRAM:

People used to strive for ways to find food. As the world advanced, we have so much of food that we don't know how to stop consuming it. That's where diet programs come in. The market is now congested with different dietary programs, all making claims of being the best. But few have achieved the heights that Weight Watchers has. And to know the secret behind Weight Watchers success we take an in-depth look into what makes it stand out.

We human beings live of motivation, without it we do not go far. Our surroundings play a vital role in that. That's what makes Weight Watchers so keen on providing you with the perfect community. People whom you can get motivated from and whom you motivate. People from different walks of life come into meetings where they share their successes and their failures providing them with the perfect encouragement to carry on with their diets. So often many of us do not have either the time or the right people around us to support us when we stand on the scale and feel broken by the number we see displayed. The community and its active meetings provide the perfect antidote for all these mental challenges that every overweight man and woman faces.

Evolution is what has kept us human beings the dominating creature. And this precise idea is what Weight Watchers have used to keep them on top. Weight Watchers introduces new and different ways to deal with so many of our daily problems. People who cannot attend meetings for any certain reasons can make use of the online forums, message boards and support groups. The newly introduced point system is also an example of how easy they make dieting for people who do not have time to calculate every single calorie they are consuming. The website itself is a dieter's heaven having everything an honest dieter would need to keep him in check and informed.

Weight Watchers is a great dieting program that is going to help you to lose weight in a safe and effective way. While other diet programs focus on really limiting your calories and telling you what you are allowed to eat and what you should stay away from. While this may work for some people, it can be a big challenge to always be kept away from some of their favourite foods. Plus making food purchases can be difficult on some of the diet plans.

Weight Watchers is going to work a bit differently. It realizes that you have a lot going on in life and you won't be able to sit around and purchase expensive products or go after hard to find ingredients in order to stay healthy. This one is based on the Smart Points that will allow you to eat the foods that work the best for you, but it does reward the healthy foods and discourages the unhealthy foods.

This plan is all about being conscious about your personal eating choices. You will be given a certain amount of points that you are able to use each day, and you get to choose how you use them up. Each of the foods that you choose will have a different point value assigned to it, and you can even make your own recipes and figure out the point values.

This program does allow you to have a bit of cheating throughout the week if you are really craving it or you are not able to resist for a big party. You will find that you can place these into your points values for the day and still eat them. As long as you are smart about some of the choices that you are making for the rest of the day, these little cheats are not going to ruin the hard work that you put in.

In addition to worrying about the healthy foods that you should consume during the week, there are other parts that come with Weight Watchers. These include going to the meetings and getting more activity into your daily life.

Acknowledging the fact that exercise is a very primal factor in having a fit body is one of the positive points of Weight Watchers too. The program changes the way people perceive health from only being related to what you eat to being related to what you exercise as well. The program also works at changing how people think about health and food in general. Making them aware of the rights and wrongs of their daily routines.

Eating on Weight Watchers is easier than you are going to find on many of the other diet plans. While these other diet plans tell you exactly what you can eat and what you should avoid, Weight Watchers takes a slightly different approach. They don't expressly tell you that you can't have any type of food because they know that life happens. They know that you aren't going to make it through the holidays without having some treats and they know that sometimes you just have a bad day and need to cheat a bit.

This is a normal life. We all have those times when it is just too hard to stay on a diet plan, and we need something that is not all that healthy for us. And this is why Weight Watchers doesn't forbid any type of food like the other diet plans; it simply gives us the tools that we need to make healthy choices. We are allowed to have that cookie on occasion, and it will fit into our points, as long as we made other healthy choices along the way.

Why Choose Weight Watchers?

There are a lot of great diet plans that you can choose to go with. Some are going to choose to have you limit your carb intake while others are going to limit the fats. Some are healthy while others are going to be hard to maintain because they are so hard on the body. Weight Watchers is a bit different than all of these because you get some options. Some of the reasons that you should choose to go with Weight Watchers instead of another weight loss program includes:

- Lose more weight—overall, people who go on a program similar to Weight Watchers are able to lose more weight than with other options. This is because it is flexible to follow and you have that motivation and support going to the meetings each week.

- Flexibility—there is a lot of flexibility that comes with being on Weight Watchers. You get to enjoy the ability to pick the foods that you want to consume, when you want to eat them and even how much, based on the amount of points that you are allowed. You can also pick your activity levels, your meetings, whether to have the meetings in person or online and so much more! This makes it easier for everyone to find the path on this plan that works best for them.

- Lifestyle change—Weight Watchers is not just about losing weight. It is about making changes in your whole lifestyle that will result in healthy weight loss. You are going to learn how to eat foods that are healthier and full of nutrition while getting rid of the foods that are causing weight gain and health issues. You are going to learn how important activity is in your life and start to implement it in more. You will work on getting healthier stress levels and sleeping as well.

- Eat the foods you like—you are the one in charge of the foods that you eat on this diet plan, so you can eat some of your favourites as well. While you do need to make some healthier choices when it comes to staying within your points, there is still the option of having some of your favourite meals on occasion.

- Ability to fit it into your daily life—it is possible to fit this diet plan into your daily life. You are able to eat real foods, foods that taste good, and will fill you up. You can choose to work out each day or do normal activities, such as chores, around the house, without having to spend hours at the gym each day. The foods can be your normal favourites as long as you are careful about not eating too much.

- You can eat out—when you are on this plan, you are allowed to eat out. While you shouldn't do this each day, eating out every once in a while is not a sin of this diet plan. It realizes that there are times you will go out with friends and family and realizing that you can go out as long as you make the right decisions for the rest of the day and don't overdo it with eating at the restaurant, you will be fine without ruining all your hard work.

- People to help you along the way—there are weekly meetings that you can attend that will help you to stay on your plan. You can meet with others who will motivate you along your journey and will help you any time that things get tuff or you need some help. It is hard to find this kind of motivation on the other diet plans that you pick.

There is no diet plan that is the same as Weight Watchers for all the flexibility and support that you are going to get along the way. If you have been trying to lose weight in the past and are ready to take that step to seeing a lot of success finally, make sure to check out Weight Watchers and see how it can work for you.

FreeStyle   2019

Based on the successful SmartPoints® system, WW Freestyle offers more than 200 zero Points® foods—including eggs, skinless chicken breast, fish and seafood, corn, beans, peas, and so much more—to multiply your meal and menu possibilities. And it makes life simpler, too: You can forget about weighing, measuring, or tracking those zero Points foods.

Total   flexibility

And because we recognize that every day is different—and some days are *really* different (think parties, business travel, holiday open houses....)—we've made your SmartPoints Budget more flexible than ever. Up to 4 unused daily SmartPoints can now roll over into your weekly SmartPoints to give you a bigger "bank" to use whenever and however you like.

How It Works

- For those of you not already familiar with SmartPoints, the SmartPoints system uses the latest nutritional science to make healthy eating as simple as possible. It nudges you toward making healthy choices so eat better and lose weight.

- Every food and drink has a SmartPoints value: a number that is based on calories, protein, sugar and saturated fat. The baseline SmartPoints value is based on the food's calories. Protein lowers the SmartPoints value. Saturated fat and sugar increase the SmartPoints value.

- Every day you get a SmartPoints Budget to spend on any foods you want.
- Your Daily SmartPoints Budget is calculated based on your age, height, weight and gender with a minimum daily value of 23.
- You only need to track the foods that have a SmartPoints value.
- You don't need to weigh, measure or track 0 SmartPoints foods.
- Enjoy a greatly total list of 0 SmartPoints go-to foods at the end of this book.
- Every week you also get a Weekly SmartPoints Budget that you can think of as "overdraft" protection. They are there to use when you go over your Daily SmartPoints budget.
- You can roll over up to four (4) unused Daily SmartPoints into your Weekly SmartPoints. Use them or not as you see fit.

Rollover Points

With the new Weight Watchers Freestyle plan for 2018, you will be able to roll over up to 4 SmartPoints daily if you do not use them.

I love this idea since it means you could adjust your points to match the natural rhythms and fluctuations of your appetite.

Here are some of the latest recipes available so you can try out the Freestyle program

- ***Being Healthy***

During a research carried out in 2007, half of the target population said their major reason for losing weight was to improve their health. When obese, one is at a risk of developing heart disease, stroke as well as cancer.

- ***Mood***

Why is this so? When one is overweight, he or she has insecurities that lead to depression as well as low self-esteem. Moreover, there is also some evidence that disorders related to one's mood and obesity is connected. Also, depression and bipolar disorder may be a precursor to obesity. Past studies have also proved that losing weight leads to improved mood.

- ***Fitness***

This is true especially for men who are regarded as being overweight.

- ***Wanting to have children***

This is because being overweight can lead to infertility and other complications during pregnancy. As we delve further into weight loss, the amount of weight you need to shed isn't really an important thing as such. You really need to know your real reasons for wanting to lose weight. We may have several reasons for wanting to shed weight, but we may not really realize what they are. When people are asked why they need to lose weight, most of them say: they want to be fit and healthy, they want to be confident, respected, love and so forth.

Consequently, you may start feeling trapped by your weight. You will start being obsessed about what you eat and the amount of exercise you do. There may be people who are leaner than you, but they are less confident, feel less loved and respected. Please be careful to lose weight for the correct reasons. If you have some solid reason for losing weight, you will definitely stick to your diet plan. There are good reasons as well as bad reasons for losing weight. The bad reasons may make you lose weight, but they will not be good enough for a long-term change in one's habits and lifestyle.

Good reasons for losing weight revolve around you while the negative ones revolve around pleasing other people such as:

- Shedding weight so as to attract someone

This may be a great trigger for weight loss; looking nice for someone you would want to be with. However, ask yourself what happens if this person does not exist in your life anymore? You will definitely lose your motivation for losing weight.

- Weight loss to boost health

This will be about you and it does not depend on what someone else thinks, says or does.

- Being referred to as overweight

Insults could motivate you to change your appearance. However, you don't need to change so as to impress someone.

In short, losing weight needs to be about you and nobody else. This is the only way to maintain your motivation and be focused on your goals.

Many people, including you, who is reading this, don't understand the main reasons why they want to lose weight. Your reasons for weight loss should be deeper and meaningful; they need to originate from your inner self. As soon as you have your valid reasons for losing weight, jot them down on an index card. Place them by your bedside and read them when you wake up and before retiring to bed.

Furthermore, you can also keep a copy at work and another in your wallet as a constant reminder of your goals.

You should also know that weight-loss goals, determine the difference between success and failure. Goals that are well-planned will keep you focused and motivated. Goals that are not realistic and overly ambitious will definitely undermine your efforts. Below are tips on losing weight:

- Concentrate on process goals

An outcome goal could be what you hope to achieve in the end. Even though this goal may give you a target, it does not guide you on how to achieve it. A process goal is a vital step in achieving whatever you desire. For instance, a process goal could be eating five portions of fruits or veggies on a daily basis, walking for half an hour daily or maybe drinking water after every meal. Process goals are particularly helpful when losing weight because you will focus on changing behaviors and habits that are important in weight loss.

- Set smart goals
1. They need to be specific- a good goal needs to have specific details.
2. They need to be measurable- if you can measure a goal, then you can objectively determine how successful you are at achieving the goal.
3. They need to be achievable- For instance, if your schedule doesn't allow you to spend an hour at the gym, then this is an unattainable goal.
4. They need to be realistic
- Your goals also need to be track-able
- Have long-term and short-term goals
- Don't try to be perfect

Setbacks are a natural part of behavior change. No one who is successful has never experienced setbacks. Identify potential barriers.

- Reassess and adjust goals as required

My Favorite Freestyle Recipes

0FS POINTS – GREEKSTYLE CHICKPEA SALAD

Nutrition Information
- Serves: 8 servings
- Serving size: ½ cup
- Calories: 192
- Fat: 4 g
- Saturated fat: 1 g
- Carbohydrates: 32 g
- Sugar: 6 g
- Fiber: 8 g
- Protein: 10 g

    [4 PointsPlus |3 Smartpoints | 0 Freestyle Points] per serving

INGREDIENTS
- 2 (15 ounce) cans chickpea, drained and rinsed
- 1 small tomato, chopped
- ¼ cup finely chopped red onion
- ½ teaspoon sugar
- ¼ cup reduced fat crumbled feta cheese
- ½ tablespoon lemon juice
- ½ tablespoon red wine vinegar
- 1 tablespoon plain nonfat Greek Yogurt
- 2 cloves garlic, minced
- ¼ teaspoon salt
- ¼ teaspoon pepper
- 1-2 tablespoons cilantro

INSTRUCTIONS
1. Drain and rinse the chickpeas and place in a medium bowl.
2. Toss in the rest of the ingredients until chickpeas are evenly coated and all of the ingredients are mixed well.
3. Serve immediately and refrigerate any leftovers.

0FS POINTS - GRILLED SHRIMP MARINADE

(Prep time: 10 min | Cook time: 10 min | Total time: 20 min | Serves: 5)

Ingredients
- 24 Medium Shrimp cleaned and deveined
- 2 teaspoons balsamic vinegar
- 1 teaspoon olive oil
- Juice of 1 Lemon
- 1 clove garlic minced
- ½ teaspoon salt
- ½ teaspoon pepper
- Pinch of red pepper flakes
- Sauce:
- 1 tablespoon prepared horseradish sauce
- 2 tablespoons ketchup
- 1 tablespoon non-fat plain Greek yogurt

Instructions
1. In a medium bowl, mix together vinegar, oil, lemon juice, garlic, salt, pepper, and pepper flakes.
2. Pour over shrimp then covers and refrigerate for a minimum of half an hour.
3. Slide shrimp onto skewers.
4. Grill for 2-3 minutes on each side. Shrimp cooks fast, so watch for it to curl and turn pink.
5. For Sauce:
6. In a small bowl, mix together all ingredients.
7. Add more or less horseradish sauce to taste

(3 PointsPlus | 2 SmartPoints | 0 SmartPoints on FreeStyle Plan or FlexPlan)

0FS POINTS - VEGETARIAN CHILI IN INSTANT POT

(Prep time: 5 min | Cook time: 25 min | Total time: 30 min | Serves: 8)

Ingredients
- 1 can black beans
- 1 can kidney beans
- 1 can refried beans
- 1 large can diced tomatoes (20 oz)
- 1 onion, diced
- ½ orange bell pepper, diced
- ½ yellow bell pepper, diced
- ½ green bell pepper, diced
- 5 cups water
- 2 vegetable bouillon cubes
- ½ teaspoon black pepper
- ½ teaspoon cayenne pepper
- 2 tablespoons chili powder
- 2 teaspoons garlic powder
- 2 teaspoons onion powder
- 1 teaspoon dried oregano
- 1 teaspoon salt (more to taste)

Instructions
1. Turn Instant Pot to Sauté function and add in oil and diced onion and bell peppers. Cook for 5 minutes or until they begin to become tender.
2. Add in black beans, pinto beans, diced tomatoes, and refried beans.
3. Add in all seasonings and water.
4. Stir well to combine.
5. Place lid on Instant Pot and set to seal.
6. Cook on Manual High Pressure for 15 minutes.
7. NPR for 10 minutes.
8. Serve with optional toppings of diced green onion, cilantro, lime wedges, sour cream, avocado

(2 PointsPlus | 1 SmartPoints | 0 SmartPoints on FreeStyle Plan or FlexPlan)
Each serving is approximately 2 cups.

0FS POINTS - MEXICAN CHICKEN SOUP

(Prep time: 15 min | Cook time: 6 H | Total time: 6 H 15 min | Serves: 10)

Ingredients
- 2 cups salsa chicken shredded
- 1 small onion chopped
- 2 cloves garlic crushed
- 1 20 ounces can crushed tomatoes
- 1 12 ounces can great northern beans
- 1 12 ounces can red kidney beans
- 1 cup frozen whole kernel corn
- 6 cups fat-free chicken stock
- 1 tablespoon cumin
- 1 teaspoon garlic powder
- 1 teaspoon onion powder
- 1 teaspoon paprika
- 1 teaspoon chili powder
- 1 teaspoon black pepper
- 1 teaspoon salt

Instructions
1. Mix all ingredients together in large Crockpot.
2. Cook on low heat for 6 hours or high heat for 3 hours.
3. Serve alone or with tortilla chips or strips as desired.

(6 PointsPlus | 5 SmartPoints | 0 SmartPoints on FreeStyle Plan or FlexPlan)

0FS POINTS - ZERO POINTS BEAN SOUP:

(12 approximately 1 cup servings)

Ingredients:
- 2 cans white beans (rinsed and drained)
- 2 cans Lima beans (rinsed and drained)
- 2 cans corn kernels drained
- 1 carton low sodium vegetable broth
- 12 slices Canadian Bacon chopped into small pieces
- Season to taste,

Directions:
1. Dump all ingredients into a large crockpot.
2. Stir gently to evenly mix ingredients.
3. Cook on low 6-8 hours. This is zero points...you have enough left for cornbread!

[5 PointsPlus |4 Smartpoints | 0 Freestyle Points] per serving

1FS Points - Chicken Taco Soup Recipe

Prep time: 5 mins
Cook time: 30 mins
Total time: 35 mins
Serves: 8

Ingredients
- 2 Cups Shredded or Cubed Chicken
- 1 onion, diced
- 1 bell pepper, diced
- 1 poblano pepper, diced
- 2 tomatoes, chopped
- 1 tablespoon garlic, minced
- 6 cups fat free chicken broth
- 1 cup tomato sauce
- 1½ cups kidney beans or pinto beans
- 2 tablespoons taco/fajita seasoning
- 1 tablespoon olive oil

Instructions
1. In a large stockpot, sauté the onion, bell pepper, poblano pepper, and tomato for 5 minutes stirring regularly. You want the vegetables to be tender.
2. Mix in chicken, broth, tomato sauce, garlic, pinto beans, and seasonings.
3. Simmer on medium heat for 30 minutes, stirring occasionally.
4. Serve with preferred garnishes like cheese, sour cream, or tortilla chips.

WW Information:
Makes 8 Servings (approximately 2 cups each)
[5 PointsPlus | 3 Smartpoints | 1 Freestyle Points] per serving

1FS Points - Sweet & Sour Turkey Meatballs

Prep time: 5 mins, Cook time: 15 mins, Total time: 20 mins

Ingredients
- 1 pound 99% Ground Turkey breast or Ground Chicken Breast
- ½ Teaspoon Salt
- 1 Teaspoon Black Pepper
- 1 Teaspoon Onion Powder
- 1 Teaspoon Garlic Powder
- 1 Teaspoon Paprika
- 1 Teaspoon Cumin
- ¼ teriyaki sauce
- ¼ Cup Sugar-Free BBQ Sauce
- ⅛ cup apple cider vinegar
- 1 tablespoon brown sugar twin

Instructions
1. In a large bowl, mix together ground meat and spices (salt, pepper, onion powder, garlic powder, paprika, and cumin). Mix until well blended.
2. In a small bowl, mix together the teriyaki sauce, BBQ sauce, apple cider vinegar, and brown sugar twin.
3. Add ¼ cup of sauce mixture to meat mixture and mix well.
4. Roll meat mixture into 1½" balls. Should make about 12 meatballs
5. Place meatballs on a lined baking sheet (we use silicone baking mats) about 1" apart
6. Bake at 375 degrees for 10 minutes. Turn meatballs, and cook for additional 10 minutes.
7. Remove from oven and toss with sauce until well coated.

WW Information:
Makes 6 servings of 3 meatballs per serving
1 SmartPoint on FreeStyle Plan or Flex Plan

2FS Points - Tasty BBQ Apricot Chicken

Prep time: 5 mins, Cook time: 30 mins, Total time: 35 mins

Ingredients
- 1 pound boneless skinless chicken breasts
- ½ cup sugar-free apricot jam
- ½ cup G Hughes Sugar Free BBQ Sauce
- 2 tablespoons low sodium soy sauce
- 1 teaspoon garlic powder
- 1 teaspoon onion powder
- 1 teaspoon ground ginger

Instructions
1. In a medium bowl, whisk together the jam, bbq sauce, soy sauce, and seasonings.
2. Line baking sheet with foil and place chicken breasts in even layer
3. Pour barbecue sauce over chicken making sure well covered.
4. Bake at 350 degrees for 30 minutes.
5. Remove from oven, and serve with favorite sides.

WW Information:
Makes 6 Servings (approximately 3oz each)
2 SmartPoints per serving on Freestyle or FlexPlan

2FS Points - Grilled Cream Corn

Prep time: 5 mins, Cook time: 20 mins, Total time: 25 mins
Makes 8 servings Each Serving is approximately ⅓ cup 10 PointsPlus per Serving 11 SmartPoints per Serving on Beyond the Scale 2 SmartPoints per Serving on FreeStyle Plan or FlexPlan

Ingredients
- 16 oz. bag frozen sweet corn
- ½ cup fat-free mayonnaise
- ¼ cup grated Parmesan cheese
- ½ cup plain non-fat Greek yogurt
- ½-¾ tsp. cayenne pepper
- ½-¾ tsp. black pepper

Instructions
1. Combine corn, mayonnaise, Parmesan cheese, Greek yogurt, cayenne pepper, and black pepper in a large bowl stir well until all ingredients are combined thoroughly.
2. Place in grill-safe cooking pan or dish and cover tightly with aluminum foil.
3. Heat on the top shelf of the grill. The bottom is fine if you don't have 2 racks,
4. Cook for 5-7 minutes or until heated through and all ingredients melted.
5. Oven instructions:
6. Preheat oven to 375 degrees and spray pan with nonstick spray.
7. Mix all ingredients together in a large bowl and pour into prepared pan.
8. Bake at 375 for 20 minutes.

2FS Points - Greek Yogurt Egg Omelet

Serves: 4

Ingredients
- 3 large eggs + three egg whites
- 2 tablespoons plain fat-free Greek yogurt
- ⅛ teaspoon salt
- ¼ teaspoon pepper
- 1 cup chopped broccoli florets
- ¼ cup finely diced onion
- ½ cup cooked and cubed ham
- ¼ cup finely chopped peppers

- 2 cups baby spinach leaves
- ¼ cup freshly grated Parmesan cheese
- 1 sliced green onion for garnish

Instructions
1. Preheat the oven to 400°F
2. Add the eggs, yogurt, salt, and pepper to a bowl. Using a hand mixer, beat until blended and frothy.
3. Spray a 10" nonstick skillet with nonstick cooking spray and turn the heat on medium-high.
4. When the pan is hot, add the broccoli, onions, peppers and ham.
5. Turn the heat down to medium, and cook the vegetables until they are tender to your liking. I cooked mine for five minutes. Keep in mind that they'll cook a little longer in the oven.
6. Add the spinach and cook until just wilted.
7. Sprinkle the green onions into the egg mixture.
8. Pour the egg mixture into the pan, making sure to get it as even as possible.
9. Sprinkle the Parmesan cheese over the eggs.
10. Let cook for approximately one minute on the stove, and then transfer the pan to the oven.
11. Bake for 10 to 15 minutes or until the eggs set.
12. Serve with additional Parmesan cheese and green onions on top.

2FS Points - Mashed Sweet Potatoes

Prep time: 5 mins, Cook time: 15 mins, Total time: 20 mins
Makes 4 Servings 2 SmartPoint per serving on FreeStyle Plan or Flex Plan

Ingredients
- 2 Large Sweet Potatoes (Washed, peeled and cubed)
- ½ Cup Plain Fat-Free Greek Yogurt
- 1 Teaspoon Garlic Powder
- ½ Teaspoon Salt
- ½ Teaspoon Cracked Black Pepper

Instructions
1. Place sweet potatoes in large saucepan and cover with water.
2. Bring to a boil over medium-high heat and cook for 8-10 minutes or until fork tender.
3. Remove from heat and drain
4. Pour into large bowl, add in yogurt and seasonings and mash until smooth.
5. We recommend using a hand mixer for the smoothest potato mixture.

3FS Points - Savory Chicken Dump Soup

3 FreeStyle Smart Points per serving (approximately 12 servings / 1 cup each)

Ingredients:
- 1 pound (approx. 3-4) raw skinless boneless chicken thighs
- 1 pkg Trader Joe's frozen Multigrain Blend with Vegetables (if you don't have a TJ's first of all bless your heart.

- Second find another frozen mix with some similar combo to this: cooked grain barley, corn, spelt [wheat], whole rice ermes variety [red], whole rice ribe variety, whole rice-venus variety [black], salt), peas, carrots, water, zucchini, vinegar, extra virgin olive oil, onion, sugar, salt, pepper and totaling no more than 17 SP for the entire bag
- 2 cups (one small package) shredded cabbage
- 1 cup (one small carton fresh or one can) sliced mushrooms any type
- 6 cups water
- 2 tsp dry Italian seasoning

Directions
1. This first part I prep ahead and have on hand in the freezer for easy dumping. If you are anxious to try this right away though there is no need to wait! Just plan a little extra time so your family and friends don't pass out smelling all that yumminess while they stalk you in the kitchen with empty bowls in hand.
2. Add all of the chicken and 1/2 the water to a tall stock pot.
3. Bring everything to a boil for 10 minutes. Reduce to a heavy simmer (not boiling, but bubbling vigorously) and cover loosely with aluminum foil. Let simmer for approximately an hour.
4. Remove one thigh and test with a meat thermometer. If the internal temp is not at least 150 (you want 165 when everything is done!) return and continue simmering for 15 minute intervals until chicken is completely done. If you are making this for prep, remove from heat and allow to cool.
5. Pull chicken apart with two forks to shred or use a hand mixer to "shred" (I haven't used the hand mixer method but I want to try it!).
6. Return to the broth you have just made and then transfer all to a freezer safe container. If you are using immediately return everything to the stock pot and go to the next step.
7. With your stock and shredded chicken in the stock pot, next dump all of the remaining ingredients and stir.
8. Bring back up to a low boil for 10 minutes, then reduce heat and simmer for 30-45 minutes

4FS points - Bruschetta Topped Balsamic Chicken

Yield: 4 SERVINGS

INGREDIENTS:

- 4 (6 oz.) raw boneless skinless chicken breasts or cutlets
- Salt and pepper, to taste
- ½ teaspoon dried oregano
- 2 teaspoons olive oil, divided
- ¾ cup balsamic vinegar
- 2 tablespoons sugar

- ¼ teaspoon salt
- 1 cup chopped cherry or grape tomatoes
- 1-2 tablespoons of sliced fresh basil
- 1 teaspoon minced garlic (or more to taste)

DIRECTIONS:

1. Pre-heat the oven to 400 degrees. Place the chicken breasts on a cutting board and if necessary, pound with a meat mallet to ensure an even thickness.
2. Sprinkle each breast with salt, pepper and oregano on each side.
3. Pour 1 ½ teaspoons of olive oil into a large skillet and bring over medium-high heat.
4. Place the breasts in the pan in a single layer and cook for 1-2 minutes on each side to lightly brown the outside of the chicken.
5. Mist a baking sheet with cooking spray and place the chicken breasts onto the sheet. Cover with aluminum foil and bake for 15 minutes.
6. While the chicken is baking, combine the balsamic vinegar, sugar and salt in a small saucepan and stir to combine. Bring to a boil over medium-high heat and then reduce the heat to medium low. Simmer for 10-15 minutes until the mixture has reduced and thickened and will coat the back of a spoon. Split the balsamic glaze into two small dishes.
7. When the chicken comes out of the oven, discard any extra liquid produced by the chicken. Use a pastry brush to brush the glaze from one of the dishes onto the chicken breasts. Place the baking sheet of chicken back in the oven, uncovered this time, for 5-10 minutes until the chicken is cooked through. Wash your pastry brush thoroughly.
8. Combine the chopped tomatoes, sliced basil, minced garlic and the remaining ½ teaspoon of olive oil in a bowl and add salt and pepper to taste. Stir to combine.
9. When the chicken breasts are done cooking, brush the second dish of balsamic glaze over the chicken breasts. Serve each breast topped with ¼ cup of the bruschetta tomato mixture.

WEIGHT WATCHERS FREESTYLE SMARTPOINTS:
4 per serving (*SP calculated using the recipe builder on weightwatchers.com*), a serving had 7 SP on the previous program

NUTRITION INFORMATION:
293 calories, 18 g carbs, 17 g sugars, 7 g fat, 1 g saturated fat, 39 g protein, 1 g fiber .

4FS POINTS - VEGAN STUFFING SOUP

Prep time: 5 mins, Cook time: 12 mins, Total time: 17 mins

Serves: 10

Ingredients

- 5 cups Pepperidge Farm Cubed Stuffing (unseasoned)
- 3 cups fat-free vegetable broth
- ¼ cup reduced-fat vegan butter or margarine, melted
- 2 tablespoons dry Vegetable Soup Mix
- 2 cloves minced garlic
- 2 teaspoons onion powder
- 2 teaspoons dried sage
- 1 teaspoon dried marjoram

Instructions

1. Preheat oven to 325 degrees
2. Spray a casserole dish with non-stick spray.
3. In a large bowl, mix together stuffing, broth, melted margarine, garlic, onion, sage, and marjoram.
4. Pour into casserole dish.
5. Bake at 325 for 12 minutes or until heated through.

4FS Points - African Sweet Potato Stew

Ingredients:

- 1 ¼ lbs. (4 to 5 cups) peeled and cubed sweet potatoes
- 2 (10 oz. each) cans diced tomatoes & green chiles (I use one regular and one mild, Ro-Tel brand.)
- 1 (16 oz.) can red beans, drained & rinsed
- 1 (14.5 oz.) vegetable broth (or chicken broth)
- ½ c. water
- 1 medium onion, chopped
- 1 medium red bell pepper, chopped
- 2 cloves garlic, minced or pressed
- 1 tsp. fresh ginger or ginger paste OR ½ tsp. ground ginger
- ½ tsp. salt
- 1 tsp. cumin
- ¼ tsp. black pepper
- 3 T. creamy peanut butter

Instructions:

1. Combine first 12 ingredients (all except peanut butter) in a slow cooker.

2. Cover and cook on low for 7-8 hours or high for 4 hours, until vegetables are tender.
3. Spoon ½ cup cooked stew liquid into a small bowl. Add peanut butter to liquid and whisk until well combined. Stir mixture into the stew.
4. Garnish each serving with chopped dry roasted peanuts (trust me on this – it's good!) and lime .
5. Weight Watchers info: This recipe makes 8 servings at 5 SmartPoints each. The serving size is 9 ounces (weight) or about 1 cup.
6. 1 ¼ lbs. (4 to 5 cups) peeled and cubed sweet potatoes
7. 2 (10 oz. each) cans diced tomatoes & green chiles (I use one regular and one mild, Ro-Tel brand.)

Weight Watchers Info:
Makes 8 servings at 9 ounces (about a cup) per serving.
Old SmartPoints: 5 SmartPoints.
Freestyle plan: 4 SmartPoints.

5FS Points - Creamy-Tomato-Basil-Soup

Serves: 4

Ingredients
- 1 cup low sodium chicken broth (or vegetable broth if you prefer)
- 1 14 oz. can tomato puree
- 1 cup skim milk
- 4-5 leaves fresh basil
- 3 tsp. olive oil
- 1 stalk celery
- ½ cup onions
- 1 Tbsp. cornstarch
- 1-2 cloves garlic, crushed.
- pepper to taste

Instructions
1. Rough chop onions and celery, transfer them to a food processor or chopper and puree until fine.
2. Heat olive oil in a large pan over medium heat.
3. Add onion and celery mix to pan and sauté until they begin to become translucent.
4. Reduce heat to low and stir in garlic, pepper, chicken stock, and tomato puree, and cornstarch-simmer on low for 5 minutes.
5. Whisk in tomato puree and milk, top with basil leaves, simmer for an additional 10 minutes.

6. Serve topped with a dollop of Greek yogurt or a fresh chopped basil.
7. This makes approximately 4 -1/2 cup servings

Makes 2 large servings

[6 PointsPlus |5 Smartpoints | 5 Freestyle Points] per serving

5FS Points - Roasted Sweet Potato Side Dish

Prep time: 5 mins, Cook time: 25 mins, Total time: 30 mins

Ingredients
- 2 Medium Sweet Potatoes
- ½ teaspoon salt
- Non-Stick Cooking Spray

Instructions
1. Preheat oven to 400 degrees.
2. Line baking sheet with silicone baking mat or spray with non-stick spray.
3. Clean sweet potatoes, and peel if desired. We usually leave the skin intact. Remove any blemishes or eyes if needed.
4. Slice sweet potatoes into ¼" thick medallions
5. Place sweet potatoes in a single layer on prepared baking sheet.
6. Sprinkle the tops lightly with salt.
7. Bake at 400 degrees for 15 minutes. Turn sweet potato medallions over and bake additional 10 minutes.

This recipe makes 4 servings.
Each serving is approximately 1/2 sweet potato.

[4 PointsPlus |5 Smartpoints | 5 Freestyle Points] per serving

0FS Points - Greek Chickpea Salad

(Prep time: 10 min | Cook time: 10 min | Total time: 20 min | Serves: 8)
One serving is 1/2 cup.

Nutrition Information
- Calories: 192
- Fat: 4 g
- Saturated fat: 1 g
- Carbohydrates: 32 g
- Sugar: 6 g
- Fiber: 8 g
- Protein: 10 g

INGREDIENTS
- 2 (15 ounce) cans chickpea, drained and rinsed
- 1 small tomato, chopped
- ¼ cup finely chopped red onion

- ½ teaspoon sugar
- ¼ cup reduced fat crumbled feta cheese
- ½ tablespoon lemon juice
- ½ tablespoon red wine vinegar
- 1 tablespoon plain nonfat Greek Yogurt
- 2 cloves garlic, minced
- ¼ teaspoon salt
- ¼ teaspoon pepper
- 1-2 tablespoons cilantro

INSTRUCTIONS

1. Drain and rinse the chickpeas and place in a medium bowl.
2. Toss in the rest of the ingredients until chickpeas are evenly coated and all of the ingredients are mixed well.
3. Serve immediately and refrigerate any leftovers. I ate ours over the course of a few days and loved it every time.

(4 PointsPlus | 3 SmartPoints | 0 SmartPoints on FreeStyle Plan or FlexPlan)

0FS POINTS - CROCK POT CHICKEN CACCIATORE

(Prep time: 10 min | Cook time: 10 min | Total time: 20 min | Serves: 5)

INGREDIENTS:
- 8 bone-in, skinless chicken thighs (about 5-ounces each), fat trimmed- in the photos for this recipe, you'll notice that I actually used 5 full chicken legs (drumstick and thigh) instead
- 3/4 teaspoon kosher salt
- freshly ground black pepper
- cooking spray
- 5 garlic cloves, finely chopped
- 1/2 large onion, chopped
- 1 28-ounce can crushed tomatoes
- 1/2 medium red bell pepper, chopped
- 1/2 medium green bell pepper, chopped
- 4 ounce sliced shiitake mushrooms
- 1 sprig of fresh thyme
- 1 sprig of fresh oregano
- 1 bay leaf
- 1 tablespoon chopped fresh parsley (I omitted this)
- freshly grated Parmesan cheese, for serving (optional)

DIRECTIONS:
1. Season the chicken with salt and pepper to taste. Heat a large nonstick skillet over medium-high heat. Coat with cooking spray, add the chicken, and cook until browned- 2 to 3 minutes per side. Transfer to your slow cooker.
2. Reduce the heat under the skillet to medium and coat with more cooking spray. Add the garlic and onion and cook, stirring, until soft- 3 to 4 minutes.
3. Transfer to the slow cooker and add the tomatoes, bell peppers, mushrooms, thyme, oregano and bay leaf. Stir to combine.
4. Cover and cook on high for 4 hours or on low for 8 hours.
5. Discard the bay leaf and transfer the chicken to a large plate. Pull the chicken meat from the bones (discard the bones), shred the meat, and return it to the sauce.
6. Stir in the parsley (if using). If desired, serve topped with Parmesan cheese.

Nutritional information per serving: Calories: 220, Fat: 6g, Sat Fat: 1.5g, Cholesterol: 123mg, Sodium: 319mg, Carbohydrates: 10g, Fiber: 2g, Sugar: 6g, Protein: 31g

(5 PointsPlus | 3 SmartPoints | 0 SmartPoints on FreeStyle Plan or FlexPlan)

0FS Points - Succotash Bean Soup

(Prep time: 10 min | Cook time: 10 min | Total time: 20 min | Serves: 5)

(12 approximately 1 cup servings)

Ingredients:
- 2 cans white beans (rinsed and drained)
- 2 cans Lima beans (rinsed and drained)
- 2 cans corn kernels drained

- 1 carton low sodium vegetable broth
- 12 slices Canadian bacon chopped into small pieces

Season to taste

Instructions

Dump all ingredients into a large crockpot. Stir gently to evenly mix ingredients. Cook on low 6-8 hours. This is zero points...you have enough left for cornbread!

 (3 PointsPlus | 2 SmartPoints | 0 SmartPoints on FreeStyle Plan or FlexPlan)

0FS Points - Slow Cook Chicken Cacciatore

INGREDIENTS:
- 8 bone-in, skinless chicken thighs
- 3/4 teaspoon kosher salt
- freshly ground black pepper
- cooking spray
- 5 garlic cloves, finely chopped
- 1/2 large onion, chopped
- 1 28-ounce can crushed tomatoes
- 1/2 medium red bell pepper, chopped
- 1/2 medium green bell pepper, chopped
- 4 ounce sliced shiitake mushrooms
- 1 sprig of fresh thyme
- 1 sprig of fresh oregano,1 bay leaf
- 1 tablespoon chopped fresh parsley (I omitted this)
- freshly grated Parmesan cheese, for serving (optional)

DIRECTIONS:

1. Season the chicken with salt and pepper to taste. Heat a large nonstick skillet over medium-high heat.
2. Coat with cooking spray, add the chicken, and cook until browned- 2 to 3 minutes per side. Transfer to your slow cooker.
3. Reduce the heat under the skillet to medium and coat with more cooking spray. Add the garlic and onion and cook, stirring, until soft- 3 to 4 minutes.
4. Transfer to the slow cooker and add the tomatoes, bell peppers, mushrooms, thyme, oregano and bay leaf. Stir to combine.
5. Cover and cook on high for 4 hours or on low for 8 hours.
6. Discard the bay leaf and transfer the chicken to a large plate. Pull the chicken meat from the bones (discard the bones), shred the meat, and return it to the sauce.
7. Stir in the parsley (if using). If desired, serve topped with Parmesan cheese.

Nutritional information per serving: Calories: 220, Fat: 6g, Sat Fat: 1.5g, Cholesterol: 123mg, Sodium: 319mg, Carbohydrates: 10g, Fiber: 2g, Sugar: 6g, Protein: 31g

[5 PointsPlus |3 Smartpoints | 0 Freestyle Points] per serving

5FS Points - Chicken Marsala MeatBall

TOTAL TIME: 30 minutes

INGREDIENTS:

- 8 ounces sliced cremini mushrooms, divided
- 1 pound 93% lean ground chicken
- 1/3 cup whole wheat seasoned or gluten-free bread crumbs
- 1/4 cup grated Pecorino cheese
- 1 large egg, beaten
- 3 garlic cloves, minced
- 2 tablespoons chopped fresh parsley, plus more for garnish
- 1 teaspoon Kosher salt
- Freshly ground black pepper
- 1/2 tablespoon all-purpose flour
- 1/2 tablespoon unsalted butter
- 1/4 cup finely chopped shallots
- 3 ounces sliced shiitake mushrooms
- 1/3 cup Marsala wine
- 3/4 cup reduced sodium chicken broth

DIRECTIONS:
1. Preheat the oven to 400F.
2. Finely chop half of the Cremini mushrooms and transfer to a medium bowl with the ground chicken, breadcrumbs, Pecorino, egg, 1 clove of the minced garlic, parsley, 1 teaspoon kosher salt and black pepper, to taste.
3. Gently shape into 25 small meatballs, bake 15 to 18 minutes, until golden.
4. In a small bowl whisk the flour with the Marsala wine and broth.
5. Heat a large skillet on medium heat.
6. Add the butter, garlic and shallots and cook until soft and golden, about 2 minutes.
7. Add the mushrooms, season with 1/8 teaspoon salt and a pinch of black pepper, and cook, stirring occasionally, until golden, about 5 minutes.
8. Return the meatballs to the pot, pour the Marsala wine mixture over the meatballs, cover and cook 10 min.
9. Garnish with parsley.

NUTRITION INFORMATION
Yield: 5 servings, Serving Size: 5 meatballs with mushrooms
[7 PointsPlus |5 Smartpoints | 5 Freestyle Points] per serving
- Amount Per Serving:

Calories: 248, Total Fat: 4g, Saturated Fat: 4g

Carbohydrates: 13g, Fiber: 1.5g, Sugar: 4.5g, Protein: 21g

5FS Points - Tasty Turkey Meatball & Veggie

INGREDIENTS
- Cooking spray
- 1 onion, chopped
- 3-4 carrots, sliced or chopped
- 1 cup green beans, cut
- 2 minced garlic cloves
- 1 (24 ounce) package Jennie-O Italian style turkey meatballs
- 2 (14.5 ounce) cans beef or vegetable broth
- 2 (14.5 ounce) diced or Italian stewed tomatoes
- 1-1/2 cups frozen corn
- 1 teaspoon oregano
- 1 teaspoon parsley
- ½ teaspoon basil

INSTRUCTIONS
1. Spray large saucepan or instant pot with cooking spray.
2. Add onions, carrots, green beans and garlic and cook over medium heat 2-3 minutes.
3. Mix in remaining ingredients.
4. If cooking on a stovetop, cover and cook over medium-low heat for 20 minutes, or until meatballs are heated through.
5. -OR-
6. If using an instant pot, press the "soup" button and cook on high pressure for 15 minutes. Vent to release pressure once cooked.
7. Refrigerate or freeze leftovers.

Nutrition Information
- Serves: 8 servings
- Serving size: 1-1/2 cup soup

[6 PointsPlus |5 Smartpoints | 5 Freestyle Points] per serving

Calories: 285, Fat: 13 g, Saturated fat: 4 g, Carbs: 21 g

Sugar: 9 g, Fiber: 3 g, Protein: 19 g

5FS Points - Garlic Roasted Garbanzo Beans

Prep time: 5 mins, Cook time: 45 mins, Total time: 50 mins

Ingredients
- 1 can garbanzo beans (chickpeas)
- 1 tablespoon olive oil
- 1 teaspoon salt
- 1 teaspoon garlic powder
- ½ teaspoon paprika

Instructions
1. Preheat oven to 375° Fahrenheit.
2. Line a baking sheet with a silicone baking mat or parchment paper.
3. Drain and rinse the garbanzo beans.
4. Pat garbanzo beans dry, pour into a large bowl.
5. Toss with olive oil, salt, garlic powder, and paprika until all are well coated.
6. Spread evenly over baking sheet.
7. Bake at 375° for 20 minutes. Turn chickpeas so they are evenly roasted (use a spatula to flip them or simply stir around but make sure they are in an even layer).
8. Place back in the oven at 375° for additional 25 minutes.
9. Allow the roasted garbanzo beans to cool before storing in an airtight container for snacking.

Makes approximately 3 servings

[7 PointsPlus | 5 Smartpoints | 5 Freestyle Points] per serving

Serve per 1/2 Cup

5FS Points - Sticky Buffalo Chicken Tenders

Prep time: 10 mins, Cook time: 15 mins, Total time: 25 mins

Ingredients
- 1 pound boneless skinless chicken breasts, pounded to ½" thickness
- ¼ cup flour
- 3 eggs
- 1 cup Italian Seasoned Panko breadcrumbs
- ½ cup brown sugar
- ⅓ cup Frank's Red Hot Sauce
- ½ teaspoon Garlic Powder

- 3 tablespoons water

Instructions
1. Preheat oven to 425 degrees and spray a baking sheet with non-stick cooking spray or line with silicone baking mats.
2. Cut boneless skinless chicken breasts into strips or chunks (we find chunks hold coating better).
3. Add the chicken into a large Ziploc bag that contains just the flour. Shake to coat.
4. Place Panko breadcrumbs into a shallow bowl. In another shallow bowl, whisk eggs until combined well.
5. Dip flour coated chicken into eggs, then into Panko breadcrumbs to coat.
6. Place coated chicken on the prepared baking sheet. Spray tops with non-stick cooking spray.
7. Bake for 15 minutes for nuggets or 20 minutes for strips or until chicken is browned and cooked through.
8. While chicken is in the oven, you will make your sauce mixture.
9. In a medium saucepan, bring the brown sugar, garlic powder, water and Frank's red hot sauce to a boil. Remove from heat and stir well.
10. When chicken is cooked through, remove from the oven and toss with sauce. This will just coat the chicken.

Makes 6 Servings

[7 PointsPlus |8 Smartpoints | 5 Freestyle Points] per serving

5FS Points - Ham & Apricot Dijon Glaze

TOTAL TIME: 5 hours

INGREDIENTS:
- 1 (6 to 7 pound) Hickory smoked fully cooked spiral cut ham
- 5 tbsp. apricot preserves
- 2 tablespoons Dijon mustard

DIRECTIONS:
1. Make the glaze: Whisk 4 tablespoons of preserves and mustard together.
2. Place the ham in a 6-quart or larger slow cooker, making sure you can put the lid on. You may have to turn the ham on its side if your ham is too large.
3. Brush the glaze over the ham. Cover and cook on the LOW setting for 4 to 5 hours. Brush the remaining tablespoon of preserves over the ham the 30 minutes.

NUTRITION INFORMATION
Yield: 16, Serving Size: 3 ounces
- Amount Per Serving:

Calories: 145, Total Fat: 7g, Saturated Fat: 1.5g
Carbohydrates: 12g, Fiber: 0g, Sugar: 11g, Protein: 15g

[5 PointsPlus |5 Smartpoints | 5 Freestyle Points] per serving

6FS Points - Pimento South American Chicken

Ingredients:
2 ½ c. cooked, chopped chicken breast (chopped into about 1/2" cubes
½ c. fat free chicken broth
1 ½ c. 98% fat free cream of mushroom soup (I use Campbell's)
1 ½ c. Healthy Request Condensed cream of chicken soup
1 4-oz. jar pimentos, drained (1/2 c.)
2 4-oz. cans Hatch green chiles, chopped and drained (You can add a 3rd can if you're just crazy about chiles like I am.)
10 oz. 50% reduced fat sharp cheddar cheese
6 oz. of Doritos (by weight) toasted corn tortilla chips, slightly crushed
Pickled jalapeños, green onions, and/or cherry tomatoes for serving (optional)

Instructions:
Mix all ingredients except Doritos and cheese. In a large casserole dish (I use 9" x 13"), layer ½ of chicken mixture, then ½ of cheese, then ½ of the Doritos. Repeat the same layers once more, ending with Doritos on top. Bake at 350° for about 40-45 minutes. Cover top with foil if Doritos begin to brown too much. Serve with pickled jalapeños and/or your favorite salsa.

Weight Watchers Info.: 6 points per serving in the new Freestyle plan; makes 8 servings.

7FS Points - Pizza Lasagna Roll-Ups

Yield: 8 PIECES

INGREDIENTS:

- 8 uncooked lasagna noodles
- 15 oz. can tomato sauce
- 1 cup pizza sauce
- ½ teaspoon Italian seasoning
- 1 lb. uncooked hot Italian poultry sausage, casings removed if present (I used Wegmans patties, you can use chicken or turkey sausage)
- 2 oz. turkey pepperoni, chopped (reserve 8 slices un-chopped for topping)
- 1 (15 oz.) container fat free Ricotta cheese
- 1 (10 oz.) package frozen chopped spinach, thawed and squeezed until dry
- 1 large egg
- 2 oz. 2% shredded Mozzarella cheese

DIRECTIONS:
1. Pre-heat the oven to 350. Lightly mist a 9×13 baking dish with cooking spray and set aside.

2. Boil and salt a large pot of water and cook lasagna noodles according to package instructions. Drain and rinse with cold water. Lay noodles flat on a clean dry surface and set aside.

3. In a mixing bowl, combine the tomato sauce, pizza sauce and Italian seasoning and stir together. Set aside.

4. Place the sausage in a large skillet over medium heat and cook until browned, breaking the meat up into small pieces as it cooks. When the sausage is cooked through, add the chopped pepperoni and 1/3 cup of the tomato sauce mixture and stir to combine. Remove from heat.

5. In a mixing bowl, combine the ricotta cheese, spinach and egg and stir until well combined. Spoon 1/3 cup of the cheese mixture onto each lasagna noodle and spread across the surface leaving a little room (about ½") at the far end with no toppings. Top the cheese layer on each noodle with the meat mixture from step four, evenly dividing the meat between the noodles. Starting with one end (not the one with space at the end), roll the noodle over the filling until it becomes a complete roll. Repeat with all noodles.

6. Spoon ½ cup of the tomato sauce mixture into the prepared baking dish and spread across the bottom. Place the lasagna rolls seam down in the dish and spoon or pour the remaining sauce over top. Sprinkle the Mozzarella over the top of the rolls and place a pepperoni on each one. Cover the dish with aluminum foil and bake for 40 minutes.

[7 PointsPlus |7 Smartpoints | 7 Freestyle Points] per serving

NUTRITION INFORMATION:
289 calories, 31 g carbs, 9 g sugars, 8 g fat, 2 g saturated fat, 24 g protein, 4 g fiber

7FS points - Apple Cheddar Turkey Wraps

Yield: 1 WRAP

INGREDIENTS:
- 1 Flatout Light Original Flatbread
- 1-2 leaves green leaf lettuce, torn
- 2 oz. thinly sliced deli turkey
- 1 oz. sliced 50% reduced fat sharp cheddar cheese
- 1 ½ teaspoons apple cider vinegar
- ½ teaspoon canola oil
- ½ teaspoon honey
- A pinch of salt and pepper
- ¼ cup matchstick-sliced apple pieces
- 1/3 cup coleslaw mix

DIRECTIONS:

1. Lay the Flatout flatbread on a clean, dry surface and lay the torn lettuce down the center of the flatbread going the long way (starting at the rounded end and spreading down the length of the flatbread to the other rounded end). You can leave a bit of space at each end as you'll be folding them over, and you do not need to cover the whole flatbread, just an area down the middle. Top the lettuce with the sliced deli turkey and the cheddar cheese. *Make sure to leave an inch or so of room at each end.*

2. In a small mixing bowl, combine the vinegar, oil, honey, salt and pepper and stir until well combined. Add the apples and coleslaw and stir to coat. Lay the apple/coleslaw mixture on top of the other ingredients layered on the wrap.

3. Fold in the rounded ends of the flatbread over the filling. Then fold one of the long edges over the filling and continue to roll until the wrap is completely rolled up. Cut in half and serve.

[7 PointsPlus |8 Smartpoints | 7 Freestyle Points] per serving

NUTRITION INFORMATION:
277 calories, 26 g carbs, 8 g sugars, 9 g fat, 3 g saturated fat, 28 g protein, 10 g fiber

BREAKFASTS RECIPES

2PTS SO TASTY MEAT SOUFFLÉ

(Prep time: 10 min, Cooking time: 30 min, Servings: 2)

2 Smart Points™

Ingredients:
- 3 eggs, whisked
- A pinch of salt and black pepper
- ¼ cup milk
- 2 bacon slices, cooked and crumbled
- ½ cup sausage, cooked and ground
- ¼ cup ham, chopped
- ½ cup cheddar cheese, shredded
- 1 green onion, chopped
- 1 cup water

Directions:
1. In a bowl, mix eggs with milk, salt, pepper, sausage, bacon, green onion, ham and cheese, stir and pour into a soufflé dish.
2. Put the water in your instant pot, add the steamer basket, add the soufflé dish, cover the dish with some tin foil, cover pot and cook on High for 30 minutes.
3. Serve hot for breakfast.

Nutrition: calories 212, fat 2, fiber 4, carbs 6, protein 10

3PTS BREAKFAST TASTY QUICHE

(Prep time: 10 min, Cooking time: 30 min, Servings: 2)
3 Smart Points™
Ingredients:
- 1 cup water
- 3 eggs
- ¼ cup milk
- A pinch of salt and black pepper
- 1 tablespoon chives, chopped
- ½ cup cheddar cheese, shredded
- Cooking spray

Directions:
1. IN a bowl, mix eggs with salt, pepper, chives and milk and whisk well.
2. Wrap a cake pan with tin foil, grease with cooking spray and add the cheese into the pan.
3. Pour eggs mixture over cheese and spread evenly.
4. Add the water to your instant pot, add the steamer basket inside, add the cake pan, cover and cook on High for 30 minutes.
5. Divide between 2 plates and serve for breakfast.

Nutrition: calories 214, fat 4, fiber 2, carbs 7, protein 8

3PTS DELICIOUS MEXICAN BREAKFAST

(Prep time: 10 min, Cooking time: 26 min, Servings: 2)

3 Smart Points™

Ingredients:
- 2 eggs, whisked
- 1 small red onion, chopped
- ¼ pound sausage, ground
- 1 small red bell pepper, chopped
- 2 ounces black beans
- 2 green onions, chopped
- 2 tablespoons flour
- ¼ cup cotija cheese, shredded
- ¼ cup mozzarella cheese, shredded
- 1 tablespoon cilantro, chopped

Directions:
1. Set your instant pot on sauté mode, add red onion and sausage, stir and cook for 6 minutes.
2. In a bowl, mix eggs with flour and whisk well.
3. Add eggs to the pot and stir.
4. Also, add beans, red bell pepper, green onion, cotija and mozzarella cheese, stir a bit, cover and cook on High for 20 minutes.
5. Divide your Mexican breakfast between 2 plates, sprinkle cilantro on top and serve for breakfast.

Nutrition: calories 254, fat 5, fiber 3, carbs 7, protein 10

1PTS SIMPLE BREAKFAST PANCAKES

Serves: 2 (6 pancakes)
1 Smart Points™

Ingredients:
¾ cup whole wheat flour
⅓ Cup applesauce, unsweetened
½ cup buttermilk (low-fat) or skim milk
1 egg white, lightly beaten
Cooking spray (preferably butter flavored)
½ tablespoon baking powder
½ tablespoon cinnamon powder
1 ½ teaspoons non-calorie artificial sweetener
½ teaspoon lemon juice

Directions:
1. Start by mixing all the ingredients together until smooth. (If you are using skim milk instead of buttermilk, you can mix the lemon juice with the milk and let it stand for 5 minutes before adding it to the batter.)
2. Check whether the batter is too thick for you. If that is the case, keep adding 1 tablespoon of water as you mix until you get the desired consistency.
3. Spray a large, non-stick skillet with cooking spray, preferably butter flavored.
4. Take two heaping tablespoons of the batter and pour them into the non-stick skillet. Spread out each pancake slightly, and cook them just the way you would any other pancakes.
5. Flip the pancakes to cook on the other side. Serve.

Nutritional Information:
Calories 185, Total Fat 1.2 g, Saturated Fat 0.3 g, Total Carbohydrates 39.5 g, Dietary Fiber 6.3 g, Sugars 12.9 g, Protein 7.9 g

4PTS EGG, BACON, AND HASH BROWNS

Serves: 4, 4 Smart Points™

Ingredients:
4 hash brown patties, frozen
6 egg whites
2 large eggs
3 ounces Canadian bacon or turkey bacon, finely chopped
Cooking spray
1 tablespoon scallion (the green part), minced
⅛ Teaspoon black pepper to taste
⅛ Teaspoon table salt to taste

Directions:
1. Coat a large nonstick skillet with cooking spray.
2. Place the hash brown patties on the skillet and cook over medium heat. Start with one side and cook until they become golden brown, about 7 to 9 minutes.
3. Flip the patties on the other side and cook them until they become golden brown, about 5 minutes.
4. In the meantime, coat another large nonstick skillet with cooking spray and heat it over medium-low heat.
5. Take a large bowl and beat together the 6 egg whites, 2 eggs, chopped Canadian bacon or turkey bacon, minced scallion, the hot pepper sauce (optional), salt, and pepper. Pour the mixture into the skillet and increase the heat to medium.
6. Allow the eggs to set partially and then scramble them using a spatula. When the eggs have set properly, remove the pan from the heat and cover it with a lid until the hash browns have cooked.
7. Place one hash brown patty on each of 4 serving plates. Divide the egg mixture into 4 portions. Top each hash patty with a portion of the egg mixture, and 2 teaspoons of ketchup.
8. Season with salt and pepper if you like, and then serve.

Nutritional Information:
Calories 85, Total Fat 4.0 g, Saturated Fat 1.3 g, Total Carbohydrate 0.9 g, Dietary Fiber 0.1 g, Sugars 0 g, Protein 10.6 g

4PTS OATMEAL MUFFIN WITH APPLESAUCE

Serves: 1, 4 Smart Points™

Ingredients:

4 teaspoons non-fat milk
3 teaspoons wheat bran
3 teaspoons whole wheat flour
2 teaspoons rolled oats (not instant)
2 teaspoons brown sugar
2 teaspoons applesauce (unsweetened)
2 teaspoons egg beaters
¼ teaspoon baking powder
¼ teaspoon cinnamon powder
Cooking spray

Directions:

1. Mix all the ingredients together until just combined. Spray a container (such as a medium-sized ramekin) with nonstick cooking spray. Pour the mixture into the container.
2. Microwave on high for 1 minute or 90 seconds. Allow it to cool, and then serve.

Nutritional Information:

Calories 100, Total Fat 0.5 g, Saturated Fat 0 g, Total Carbohydrate 20.8 g, Dietary Fiber 3.2 g, Sugars 2.0 g, , Protein 3.2 g

4PTS AVOCADO AND PEAR SMOOTHIE

Serves: 4, 4 Smart Points™

Ingredients:

1 Hass avocado, ripe and firm
1 cup pear juice, unsweetened
½ cup Greek yogurt (nonfat)
2 tablespoons honey
½ teaspoon vanilla extract
2 cups ice cubes

Directions:

1. Cut the avocado in half.
2. Remove the pit and use a spoon to scoop the avocado into a blender.
3. Add the pear juice, yogurt, honey, and vanilla to the blender and puree until the mixture becomes smooth. Add the ice cubes and blend again, and you have a smoothie for your breakfast.
4. Pour the smoothie into 4 glasses and serve.

Nutritional Information:

Calories 160, Total Fat 7.4 g, Saturated Fat 2.8 g, Total Carbohydrate 3.4 g, Dietary Fiber 3.4 g, Sugars 0.6 g, Protein 4.0 g

5PTS MUFFINS WITH LEMON POPPY SEEDS

Serves: 12
5 Smart Points™

Ingredients:
- ½ cup sugar
- 2 eggs
- ¼ cup applesauce, unsweetened
- 1 teaspoon vanilla extract
- 1 large lemon, zest and juiced
- ¾ cup plain Greek yogurt (fat free)
- ½ cup white rice flour
- ½ cup oat flour
- ⅓ Cup brown rice flour
- 2 teaspoon baking powder
- ½ teaspoon baking soda
- ½ teaspoon salt
- 2 tablespoon poppy seeds
- 2 tablespoon almonds, sliced

Directions:
1. Preheat the oven to 350°F.
2. Either grease a muffin tin lightly, or line it with muffin papers.
3. In a large bowl, cream the following ingredients together: sugar, eggs, applesauce, and vanilla extract. Add the lemon zest to the mixture as well as the lemon juice and Greek yogurt. Mix all the ingredients until they are well combined.
4. Add the white rice flour, oat flour and brown rice flour, baking powder, baking soda, and salt. Mix until the ingredients have been well combined. Put in the poppy seeds and mix them with the other ingredients.
5. Divide the batter among the muffin cups. Sprinkle the almonds on top. Bake for about 20 minutes, or until you insert a toothpick at the center of each muffin, and it comes out clean.

Nutritional Information:
Calories 132, Total Fat 3.0 g, Saturated Fat 0.5 g, Total Carbohydrate 22.0 g, Dietary Fiber 1.0 g, Sugars 10.0 g, Protein 5.0 g

6PTS TASTY HASH BROWNS OMELET

Serves: 4
6 Smart Points™

Ingredients:
6 slices bacon
2 cups hash browns, frozen, or chopped potatoes
½ cup onion, chopped
½ cup green pepper, chopped
4 eggs
¼ cup milk
1 cup cheese, grated
Salt and pepper to taste

Directions:
1. Start by cooking the bacon slices in a heavy skillet until they become crispy. Remove them from the pan and set them aside to cool.
2. Mix the hash browns or chopped potatoes, onion and green pepper in the same skillet where you cooked the bacon. The pan will have bacon drippings to cook the mixture.
3. Cook over low heat until the underside of the mixture becomes brown and crispy.
4. Blend the 4 eggs with the milk and then pour this mixture over the potato mixture. Top with the grated cheese and cooked bacon.
5. Cover the skillet with a lid and cook the mixture over low heat for about 20 minutes or until the egg is cooked. Remove from the heat.
6. Cut the omelet into wedges. Sprinkle with salt and pepper to taste. Serve.

Nutritional Information:
Calories 514, Total Fat 34.9 g, Saturated Fat 12.4 g, Total Carbohydrate 30.4 g, Dietary Fiber 2.8 g, Sugars 2.4 g, Protein 19.0 g

5PTS WHOLESOME STRAWBERRY BRUSCHETTA

Serves: 4, 5 Smart Points™

Ingredients:
- 4 thick slices whole wheat bread
- 5 tablespoons light brown sugar
- 2 teaspoons lemon juice
- 3 cups fresh strawberries, diced
- 4 tablespoons cream cheese (reduced fat)

Directions:
1. Toast the 4 slices of bread in a toaster.
2. Heat a large nonstick skillet over high heat. Add the brown sugar and lemon juice. Cook, stirring regularly, until the sugar has melted. Within 30 seconds to 1 minute the mixture will start to bubble.
3. Add the fresh strawberries, stirring often until the berries are heated through and the juices come out, which should take about another 30 seconds to 1 minute. If more time is needed to get the desired results, then allow it.
4. Remove from the heat. Take each slice of toast and spread 1 tablespoon of light cream cheese on. Top with the cooked berries and enjoy.

Nutritional Information:
Calories 166, Total Fat 3.0 g, Saturated Fat 0.2 g, Total Carbohydrate 38.0 g, Dietary Fiber 4.0 g, Sugars 15.6 g, Protein 5.0 g

4PTS RAISIN BREAD WITH PINEAPPLE

Serves: 1, 4 Smart Points™

Ingredients:

1 egg (medium)
¼ cup canned pineapple (no sugar added), crushed
¼ teaspoon cinnamon powder, divided
1 slice raisin bread

Directions:

1. Beat the egg in a shallow dish. Add half of the cinnamon and combine.
2. Drain the juice from the pineapple into the egg mixture and beat it again. Prick the slice of bread with a fork on both sides and soak the slice in the egg mixture. Turn the bread many times so it can absorb a lot of egg mixture.
3. Gently transfer the slice of bread to a nonstick baking sheet. Take the drained pineapple and the remaining cinnamon powder and spread it on the bread together with the remaining egg mixture. Bake at 400°F for about 20 minutes, and serve warm.

Nutritional Information:

Calories 168, Total Fat 5.6 g, Saturated Fat 2.1 g, Total Carbohydrate 22.1 g, Dietary Fiber 1.9 g, Sugars 12.2 g, Protein 7.6 g

5PTS ENERGIZING BREAKFAST BURRITO

Serves: 4, 5 Smart Points™

Ingredients:

2 teaspoons olive oil
2 scallions, chopped
1 tomato, chopped
1 green pepper, chopped
2 garlic cloves, minced
2 large eggs
4 egg whites
2 tablespoons cilantro, chopped
½ cup cheddar cheese, chopped
¼ teaspoon salt
¼ teaspoon pepper
4 whole wheat tortillas
Cooking spray (non-fat)
½ cup sour cream (non-fat)
½ cup salsa

Directions:

1. Preheat the oven to 400°F.
2. Heat a skillet over medium heat and add the oil. When the oil has heated, add the chopped scallions, tomato, green pepper, and minced garlic. Sauté the mixture for 5 minutes. Add the whole eggs and the egg whites. Cook until the eggs are scrambled, about 3 to 5 minutes.
3. Remove from the heat and add the cilantro, cheese, salt, and pepper as you stir.
4. Spray a baking dish with cooking spray. Place one tortilla on a plate and spoon a quarter of the mixture on top. Roll up the tortilla and place it on the baking dish with the seams facing downwards. Repeat this method with the remaining tortillas.
5. Bake for 10 minutes and then serve with salsa and sour cream.

Nutritional Information:

Calories 298, Total Fat 9.3 g, Saturated Fat 2.4 g, Total Carbohydrate 36.6 g, Dietary Fiber 1.7 g, Sugars 5.4 g, Protein 17.4 g

2PTS COCONUT AND RASPBERRY SMOOTHIE

Serves: 1

2 Smart Points™

Ingredients:

1 cup vanilla coconut milk (unsweetened)

1 cup crushed ice cubes

¾ cup frozen raspberries (unsweetened)

⅛ Teaspoon coconut extract

2 packets calorie-free sweetener (i.e. Truvia or Splenda)

Directions:

1. Partially thaw the frozen raspberries.
2. Place all the ingredients in a blender and mix at high speed until smooth. Serve in a glass and enjoy.

Nutritional Information:

Calories 106, Total Fat 5.0 g, Saturated Fat 0 g, Total Carbohydrate 15.5 g, Dietary Fiber 7.5 g, Sugars 4.5 g, Protein 1.0 g

4PTS QUICK BUCKWHEAT PORRIDGE

Preparation time: 10 minutes
Cooking time: 6 minutes
Servings: 2
4 Smart Points™
Ingredients:
- 1 cup buckwheat groats, rinsed
- ¼ cup raisins
- 3 cups rice milk
- 1 banana, peeled and sliced
- ½ teaspoon vanilla extract

Directions:
1. Put buckwheat in your instant pot, add raisins, milk, banana and vanilla, stir a bit, cover and cook on High for 6 minutes.
2. Divide buckwheat porridge into 2 bowls and serve for breakfast.

Nutrition: calories 162, fat 1, fiber 2, carbs 2, protein 5

4PTS HEALTHY SQUASH PORRIDGE

Preparation time: 10 minutes
Cooking time: 8 minutes
Servings: 2
4 Smart Points™
Ingredients:
- 3 small apples cored
- 1 small delicata squash
- 1 and ½ tablespoon gelatin
- 2 tablespoon slippery elm
- ½ cup water
- 1 and ½ tablespoons maple syrup
- A pinch of cinnamon powder
- A pinch of ginger powder
- A pinch of cloves, ground

Directions:
1. Put the squash and apples in your instant pot, add water, cinnamon, ginger and cloves, cover and cook on Manual for 8 minutes.
2. Leave squash to cool down, transfer to a cutting board, halve, deseed and transfer to your blender.
3. Add apples, water and spices as well and pulse really well.
4. Add slippery elm, maple syrup and gelatin, blend well, divide into 2 big bowls and serve for breakfast.

Nutrition: calories 174, fat 2, fiber 1, carbs 3, protein 4

4PTS INSTANT ORANGE SMOOTHIE

Serves: 2

4 Smart Points™

Ingredients:

1 ¼ cups freshly squeezed orange juice

½ cup fat free milk

8 ice cubes, crushed

2 tablespoons sugar

1 teaspoon vanilla extract

Directions:

1. Combine all the ingredients including the crushed iced cubes in a blender and puree until they become smooth.
2. If the smoothie becomes too thin, add more ice cubes and puree again until you get the desired texture. Serve.

Nutritional Information:

Calories 148, Total Fat 0.0 g, Total Carbohydrate 31.0 g, Sugars 19.1 g, Dietary Fiber 0.4 g, Protein 3.5 g

5PTS FRUIT, VEGETABLE AND HERB SMOOTHIE

Serves: 2

5 Smart Points™

Ingredients:

1 cup cold water

3 cups fresh spinach leaves, chopped

2 cups lettuce, chopped

1 apple, cored and chopped

1 pear, cored and chopped

½ cup parsley, chopped

2 stalks celery

1 ripe banana, cut in pieces

½ cup orange juice, freshly squeezed

Juice of 1 lime, freshly squeezed juice

3 to 5 ice cubes, crushed

Instructions

1. Put the water, spinach, and lettuce into a blender. Start the blender on low speed and puree until smooth.
2. Gradually increase the speed to high, and add the apple, pear, parsley, and celery. Blend until smooth and then add the banana pieces, and the orange and lime juices, and ice. Serve in 2 glasses and enjoy.

Nutritional Information:

Calories 216, Total Fat 0.0 g, Total Carbohydrate 53.0 g, Sugars 34.2 g, Dietary Fiber 9.0 g, Protein 3.5 g

3PTS PEACHES AND CREAM OATMEAL DELIGHT

Preparation Time: 15 minutes, 3 Smartpoints

Ingredients:

1 peach, chopped
2 cups rolled oats
1 tsp vanilla
4 cups water
Non-dairy milk (optional)

Instructions:

Place the oats, peaches, vanilla, and water into the Instant Pot.

Press the Porridge button and set the pressure on High setting. Ensure that the lid is shut tightly and the valve is closed.

Use the Adjust button to set the timer for 3 minutes of cooking. When the timer beeps, allow for Natural Pressure Release, which should take 10 minutes, and then use Quick Pressure Release.

Pour out the oatmeal into 4 bowls. Top off with maple syrup or chopped almonds. Serve immediately.

Serves: 4

5PTS APPLE AND CRANBERRY OATMEAL

Preparation Time: 50 minutes , 5 Smartpoints

Ingredients:
- 2 cups steel cut oats
- 4 apples, diced
- 3 cups water
- 3 cups coconut milk
- 1 ½ fresh cranberries
- ½ tsp nutmeg
- 1 tsp lemon juice
- 4 Tbsp coconut oil
- ½ tsp salt
- ¼ cup maple syrup
- 2 tsp cinnamon

Instructions:
Spray coconut oil into the steel bowl of the Instant Pot.

Pour the water into the Instant Pot and add all the ingredients, except the salt and maple syrup. Soak overnight.

In the morning, stir in the syrup and salt. Close the lid and valve, and press the Porridge button to cook. This will take about 40 minutes.

When the timer beeps, use Quick Release to remove pressure.

Serve with coconut milk.

Serves: 6

3PTS CREAMY BANANA FRENCH TOAST

This is a simple and quick recipe that is perfect for a family meal. The dish looks like bread pudding, with a soft texture and delicious taste. The bananas, nuts, and syrup are great toppings, but if bananas aren't your thing, then omit them from the recipe.

Preparation Time: 40 minutes, 3 Smartpoints

Ingredients:

- 4 bananas, sliced
- 6 slices French bread, cubed
- 3 eggs
- 3 Tbsp brown sugar
- ½ cup coconut milk
- 1 tsp vanilla
- ¼ cup pecans, chopped
- ½ tsp ground cinnamon
- Maple syrup (optional)

Instructions:

Grease a baking dish that will fit inside your Instant Pot.

Place the bread cubes in the baking dish. Add a layer of sliced bananas on the bread and sprinkle 1 tablespoon of brown sugar over it.

Add the remaining bread and then another layer of sliced bananas over the bread. Sprinkle 1 tablespoon of brown sugar and half of the chopped pecans over it.

Beat the eggs in a bowl and whisk together with the coconut milk, vanilla, 1 tablespoon brown sugar, and cinnamon. Pour this mixture evenly all over the bread.

Pour a cup of water into the Instant Pot and lower in a trivet. Place the baking dish on the trivet.

Lock the lid and press the Porridge button. When the timer beeps, release pressure quickly. Remove the lid and take out the baking dish.

Allow to sit for 5 minutes, and then top off with nuts and maple syrup.

Serves: 6

4PTS LOW CARB BREAKFAST PORRIDGE

This dish will keep you warm on those wintry mornings when you don't want to spend too much time preparing grain-free porridge and aren't keen on having eggs for breakfast. The fruits make it extremely filling and healthy, and the cinnamon and honey add to the sweet flavor.

Preparation Time: 10 minutes 4 Smartpoints

Ingredients:
- 1 cup water
- ½ cup cashews, raw
- ½ cup dried coconut shreds
- ¼ cup shelled Pepitas
- 1 Tbsp honey
- ½ cup pecans, chopped
- 2 tsp coconut oil

Instructions:

Place all the ingredients into a blender, but leave out the water, honey, and coconut oil. Blend for half a minute.

Pour the contents into the Instant Pot. Add the water, honey, and oil, and stir well. Lock the lid, close the valve, and press the Porridge button. Adjust the timer to read 3 minutes and cook the meal.

Quick Release the pressure and open the lid. Stir the porridge and serve topped with fresh fruit.

Serves: 2

5PTS DAIRY-FREE PEAR OATMEAL

Preparation Time: 10 minutes, 5 Smartpoints

Ingredients:
- 1 cup rolled oats
- 2 cups pear, peeled and diced
- 2 cups almond milk
- ½ cup walnuts, chopped
- ½ cup raisins
- ¼ cup brown sugar
- ½ tsp cinnamon
- 1 Tbsp dairy-free butter, melted
- ¼ tsp salt

Instructions:
Mix all the ingredients in a heat-resistant bowl.
Lower the trivet into the Instant Pot and pour in 1 cup of water. Lower the bowl onto the trivet, secure the lid, and close the steam vent.
Press the Manual button and cook for 6 minutes.
Use Quick Release to remove the pressure.
Serve warm.
Serves: 4

CHICKEN RECIPES

6PTS CHICKEN OKRA SOUP

(Prep time: 20 min, Cooking time: 30 min, Servings: 2)

6 Smart Points™

Ingredients

- Coconut milk 120g
- Water 300g
- Curry sauce mix 1 portions
- Ground ginger 2g
- Broccoli paste 55g
- Carrots paste 55g
- Water chestnut 55g
- Frozen okra 85g
- Cooked chicken breast 8g

Preparation Method

1. Place all ingredients in instant pot cooker and select soup option.
2. That it's after a few minutes your tasty soup will be ready.

Nutritional Information

- Calories: 179
- Calories from Fat: 39
- Fat: 4.4g
- Saturated Fat: 0.7g
- Cholesterol: 0mg
- Carbohydrates: 32.2g
- Fiber: 6.5g
- Sugar: 5.1g
- Protein: 4.4g

12PTS VINEGAR CHICKEN

(Prep time: 20 min, Cooking time: 15 min, Servings: 2)
12 Smart Points™
Ingredients
- Chicken thighs 600g
- White vinegar 15g
- Fish sauce 10g
- Garlic 2 cloves
- Black peppercorns 2g
- Bay leaves 2

Preparation Method
1. Select poultry option in your instant pot cooker and add chicken including your ingredients (you don't have to sauté anything).
2. Close the lid, and cook for 15 minutes. Serve hot.

Nutritional Information
- Calories: 544
- Calories from Fat: 272
- Fat: 30.2g
- Saturated Fat: 6.7g
- Cholesterol: 142mg
- Carbohydrates: 26.6g
- Fiber: 0.8g
- Sugar: 22g
- Protein: 38.9g

9PTS CHICKEN COLA WINGS

(Prep time: 30 min, Cooking time: 17 min, Servings: 2)

9 Smart Points™

Ingredients

- Chicken wings 300g
- Garlic 2 cloves
- Green onion 1 stalk
- Sliced ginger 14g
- Coca Cola 100g
- Light soy sauce 14g
- Dark soy sauce 7g
- Rice wine 7g
- Vegetable oil 7g

Preparation Method

1. At first, select sauté mode in your instant pot cooker and add oil.
2. When oil is hot, add ginger, garlic, onions and sauté until fragrant nicely.
3. Now, add slowly chicken wings and stir approximately 2minutes or until wings are coated all sides with gravy.
4. When edges of wings turn to golden brown and immediately add coca cola, stir using a wooden spoon and add both soy sauce (dark and light), rice wine. Mix well until it combined well and select cooker cooking timer for 5 minutes on high pressure and wait for natural pressure release (approximately 10 minutes).
5. If desired, add extra seasoning (it shouldn't taste like coca cola). Serve immediately with rice or brown rice.

Nutritional Information

Calories: 280
Fat: 14.1g
Saturated Fat: 3.1g
Carbohydrates: 14.2g
Fiber: 0g
Sugar: 12.8g
Protein: 19g

6PTS HONEY SESAME CHICKEN

Serves: 4

6 Smart Points™

Ingredients:

1 pound boneless, skinless chicken breast

2 teaspoons coconut oil

½ teaspoon salt

1 teaspoon coarse ground black pepper

½ teaspoon cayenne powder

1 tablespoon freshly grated ginger

2 tablespoons honey

¼ cup soy sauce

2 teaspoons sesame oil

1 tablespoon sesame seeds, toasted (optional)

Fresh lemongrass for garnish, optional

Cooked rice for serving (optional)

Directions:

1. Using a meat mallet, flatten the chicken until it is approximately ¼ inch thick.
2. Melt the coconut oil in a skillet over medium heat.
3. Season the chicken with salt, black pepper, and cayenne powder. Cook the chicken in the skillet for 4-5 minutes per side, or until it is no longer pink in the center.
4. In a small bowl, combine the fresh ginger, honey, soy sauce, and sesame oil. Mix well and pour the sauce over the chicken. Continue cooking, just until the liquid begins to bubble, approximately 1-2 minutes.
5. Remove from the heat and serve warm, garnished with sesame seeds and lemongrass, if desired.

Nutritional Information:

Calories 210, Total Fat 7.5 g, Saturated Fat 3.1 g, Total Carbohydrate 8.9 g, Dietary Fiber 0.0 g, Sugars 8.7 g, Protein 25.9 g

3PTS TASTY ORANGE CHICKEN

Serves: 4, 3 Smart Points™

Ingredients:

2 teaspoons olive oil or cooking spray

¾ cup sweet yellow onion, sliced

1 cup red bell pepper, sliced

1 pound boneless, skinless chicken breast, cubed

½ teaspoon salt

1 teaspoon coarse ground black pepper

1 teaspoon garlic powder

¼ cup low sugar orange marmalade

2 tablespoons soy sauce

Cooked rice for serving (optional)

Directions:

1. Heat the olive oil or cooking spray in a skillet over medium heat.
2. Place the onion and red bell pepper in the skillet and cook for 3-5 minutes, or until the vegetables are just starting to become tender. Remove from the skillet and set aside.
3. Season the chicken with the salt, black pepper and garlic powder. Add the chicken to the skillet and cook, stirring occasionally, for 5-7 minutes.
4. While the chicken is cooking, combine the marmalade and soy sauce. Mix well and then add to the chicken. Toss to coat.
5. Add the vegetables back into the skillet and continue to cook for an additional 5-7 minutes, or until the chicken is cooked through.
6. Remove from the heat and serve warm with cooked rice, if desired.

Nutritional Information:

Calories 173, Total Fat 3.1 g, Saturated Fat 0.8 g, Total Carbohydrate 8.4 g, Dietary Fiber 0.9 g, Sugars 4.6 g, Protein 26.4 g

5PTS CAJUN CHICKEN AND SWEET POTATO HASH

Serves: 4, 5 Smart Points™

Ingredients:
2 teaspoons olive oil or cooking spray
4 cups sweet potatoes, peeled and shredded
1 cup sweet yellow onion, diced
1 cup red bell pepper, diced
1 teaspoon salt
1 teaspoon black pepper
1 teaspoon Cajun seasoning mix
2 cups boneless skinless chicken breast, cooked and shredded
2 cups tomatoes, chopped
Fresh scallions, sliced for garnish (optional)

Directions:
1. Heat the olive oil or cooking spray in a large skillet over medium-high heat.
2. In a bowl, combine the sweet potatoes, onion, and red bell pepper. Toss to mix.
3. Add the vegetable mixture to the skillet and cook for 5-7 minutes, stirring frequently.
4. Season the vegetables with salt, black pepper and Cajun seasoning. Using a spatula, press the vegetables firmly into the bottom of the pan. Reduce the heat to medium and let them cook, without disturbing them, for 5-7 minutes, or until a crust begins to form on the bottom of the vegetables.
4. Add the chicken and tomatoes. Toss gently to mix and cook and additional 5-7 minutes, or until the chicken is heated through and the vegetables are tender.
5. Remove from the heat and serve warm, garnished with fresh scallions if desired.

Nutritional Information:
Calories 242, Total Fat 3.6 g, Saturated Fat 0.9 g, Total Carbohydrate 24.0 g, Dietary Fiber 3.9 g, Sugars 0.8 g, Protein 28.1 g

5PTS INSTANT FAJITA CASSEROLE

Serves: 4, 5 Smart Points™

Ingredients:
- ½ teaspoon salt
- 1 teaspoon coarse ground black pepper
- 1 teaspoon cumin
- ½ teaspoon cayenne powder
- ½ teaspoon smoked paprika
- Cooking spray
- 1 pound chicken breast tenders
- 2 cups yellow and green bell peppers, sliced
- 1 cup red onion, sliced
- 1 cup stewed tomatoes, chopped, juice included
- ¾ cup queso fresco cheese, crumbled
- Fresh cilantro for garnish (optional)

Directions:
1. Combine the salt, black pepper, cumin, cayenne powder and smoked paprika. Set aside.
2. Preheat the oven to 375°F and spray an 8x8 or larger baking dish with cooking spray.
3. Arrange the chicken tenders in an even layer in the baking dish and season liberally with at least half of the seasoning mixture.
4. Place the bell peppers and onions over the chicken, followed by the stewed tomatoes.
5. Add any remaining seasoning mixture to the top of the peppers and onions.
6. Sprinkle the queso fresco cheese over the top and place the pan in the oven.
7. Bake uncovered for 25-30 minutes, or until the chicken is cooked through.
8. Remove from the oven and let sit for 5 minutes.
9. Serve warm, garnished with fresh cilantro, if desired.

Nutritional Information:

Calories 233, Total Fat 7.7 g, Saturated Fat 3.8 g, Total Carbohydrate 8.7 g, Dietary Fiber 2.0 g, Sugars 1.5 g, Protein 31.4 g

3PTS BAKED ARTICHOKE CHICKEN

Serves: 4
3 Smart Points™

Ingredients:
1 pound chicken breast tenders
Cooking spray
1 teaspoon salt
1 teaspoon coarse ground black pepper
1 cup jarred artichoke hearts
1 cup heirloom tomatoes, chopped
3 cloves garlic, crushed and minced
½ cup fresh basil, torn
1 tablespoon olive oil

Directions:
1. Preheat the oven to 375°F and spray an 8x8 or larger baking dish.
2. Place the chicken tenders in an even layer in the baking dish and season with the salt and coarse ground black pepper.
3. Combine the artichoke hearts, tomatoes, garlic, and basil in a bowl. Drizzle in the olive oil and toss to mix.
4. Spread the artichoke mixture over the chicken.
5. Place in the oven and bake for 25-30 minutes, or until the chicken is cooked through.
6. Remove from the oven and let rest at least 5 minutes before serving.

Nutritional Information:
Calories 185, Total Fat 3.2 g, Saturated Fat 0.8 g, Total Carbohydrate 8.9 g, Dietary Fiber 2.0 g, Sugars 1.5 g, Protein 28.4 g

6PTS GARLIC THAI CHICKEN

Serves: 4

6 Smart Points™

Ingredients:

1 pound chicken breast tenders

Cooking spray

¼ cup garlic chili sauce

2 tablespoons honey

1 teaspoon salt

1 teaspoon black pepper

2 cups asparagus spears, chopped

1 cup onion, sliced

1 tablespoon olive oil

Cooked rice for serving (optional)

Directions:

1. Preheat the oven to 375°F and spray an 8x8 or larger baking dish with cooking spray.
2. Place the chicken in a single layer in the baking dish and season with the salt and black pepper.
3. In a bowl, combine the garlic chili sauce and honey. Mix well.
4. Pour the sauce mixture over the chicken, using a basting brush to evenly distribute over each piece.
5. Add the asparagus and onion to the baking dish and drizzle with the olive oil.
6. Place the baking dish in the oven and bake for 25-30 minutes, or until the chicken is cooked through.
7. Remove from the oven and let rest for at least 5 minutes before serving.

Nutritional Information:

Calories 242, Total Fat 6.6 g, Saturated Fat 1.3 g, Total Carbohydrate 17.1 g, Dietary Fiber 2.6 g, Sugars 10.6 g, Protein 28.2 g

3PTS CREAMY DIJON CHICKEN

Serves: 4

3 Smart Points™

Ingredients:

1 pound boneless, skinless chicken breasts

1 tablespoon olive oil or cooking spray

1 teaspoon salt

1 teaspoon white pepper

1 teaspoon fresh thyme

¼ cup Dijon mustard

½ cup low fat milk

2 cloves garlic, crushed and minced

4 cups fresh spinach, torn

Directions:

1. Heat the olive oil in a skillet over medium heat.
2. Using a meat mallet, pound the chicken until it reaches a thickness of approximately ¼ inch.
3. Season the chicken with salt, white pepper and fresh thyme. Add the chicken to the skillet and cook for 3-4 minutes per side.
4. Combine the Dijon mustard, milk, and garlic.
5. Add the Dijon mixture to the skillet and cook for 1-2 minutes.
6. Add the spinach and cook an additional 4-5 minutes, turning the chicken occasionally, until the chicken is cooked through and the spinach is wilted.
7. Remove from heat and serve warm with favorite accompaniment.

Nutritional Information:

Calories 170, Total Fat 3.2 g, Saturated Fat 0.8 g, Total Carbohydrate 2.6 g, Dietary Fiber 0.7 g, Sugars 1.7 g, Protein 27.6 g

4PTS LIGHT CHICKEN SALAD

Serves: 3
4 Smart Points™

Ingredients:
2 pieces boneless chicken breast
2 celery stalks, finely chopped
1 chicken bouillon cube
¼ onion, chopped
3 tablespoons light mayonnaise
2 tablespoons parsley chopped

Directions:
1. Place the chicken breasts, half of the chopped celery, half the onion, and parsley in a medium saucepan. Cover the ingredients with water. Add the chicken bouillon cube, and cover with a lid.
2. Cook on medium heat for about 15 to 20 minutes, or until the chicken has cooked through. Remove the chicken from the heat and let it cool. Reserve the chicken broth.
3. Dice the chicken and place it in a bowl. Add the remaining celery, onions, and the mayonnaise. Add ⅛ cup of the chicken broth you had reserved, and mix well. Add more if the chicken looks dry. Serve on lettuce, as a lettuce wrap, or on bread.

Nutritional Information:
Calories 169, Total Fat 5.3 g, Saturated Fat 2.8 g, Total Carbohydrate 4.1 g, Dietary Fiber 1.0 g, Sugars 1.1 g, Protein 25.4 g

8PTS CHILI TURKEY MACARONI WITH JALAPENOS

Serves: 8, 8 Smart Points™

Ingredients:
- 2 teaspoon chili powder
- 1 teaspoon garlic powder
- 1 teaspoon ground coriander
- 1 teaspoon onion powder
- 1 teaspoon cumin
- ¼ teaspoon salt
- 1 tablespoon olive oil
- 1 pound ground turkey
- 3 cups beef broth
- 1 (10 ounce) can tomatoes with green chilies, diced
- 2 cups dry whole wheat elbow pasta
- ½ cup low fat milk
- 4 ounces cream cheese
- 1 cup cheddar cheese, shredded
- ½ cup pickled jalapenos, chopped

Directions:
1. In a small bowl, mix together the chili powder, garlic powder, ground coriander, onion powder, chili powder, cumin, and salt.
2. In a medium saucepan, heat the olive oil on medium-high. Add the turkey and cook until it turns color. Add the spices, mix them in, and allow the mixture to cook for a further 1 or 2 minutes. Stir in the beef broth, diced tomatoes, and dry pasta. Cover the pot and cook for about 8 to 10 minutes.
3. Before the pasta finish cooking, poor the milk in a pot and place it over low heat. When the milk is warm and steamy, mix in the cheese cream until it melts. The shredded cheese can then be added to the milk. Stir until it melts.
4. Empty the cheese sauce into the pasta blend and mix until the pasta is equally covered. Blend in the pickled jalapenos. Give it a taste and add more salt if necessary. Serve hot.

Nutritional Information:
Calories 322, Total Fat 15.0 g, Saturated Fat 4.8 g, Total Carbohydrate 20.3 g, Dietary Fiber 4.0 g, Sugars 11.2 g, Protein 20.0 g

6PTS GRILLED CHICKEN SALAD

Serves: 4, 6 Smart Points™

Ingredients:

- ¼ cup mayonnaise (low-fat)
- 1 teaspoon curry powder
- 2 teaspoons water
- 4 ounces or 1 cup rotisserie chicken,
- ¾ cup apple, chopped
- ⅓ Cup celery, diced
- 3 tablespoons raisins
- ⅛ Teaspoon salt

Directions:

1. In a medium-sized bowl, combine the mayonnaise, curry powder, and water. Stir with a whisk until well blended.
2. Add the chopped chicken, celery, raisins, chopped apple, and salt. Stir the ingredients so they get combined well. Cover the salad and chill in the fridge. Serve in a lettuce wrap, with bread, or on its own.

Nutritional Information:

Calories 222, Total Fat 5.4 g, Saturated Fat 2.1 g, Total Carbohydrate 26.9 g, Dietary Fiber 2.5 g, Sugars 8.1 g, Protein 23.0 g

4PTS TASTY CHICKEN FRIED RICE

Serves: 4, 4 Smart Points™

Ingredients:

4 large egg whites
12 ounces boneless, skinless chicken breast, cut in ½ -inch pieces
½ cup carrot, diced
½ cup scallion (green and white parts), chopped
2 garlic cloves, minced
½ cup frozen green peas, thawed
2 cups cooked brown rice, hot
3 tablespoons soy sauce (low-sodium)

Directions:

1. Coat a large, nonstick skillet with cooking spray, and set it over medium-high heat.
2. Add the egg whites and stir frequently as you cook, until they are scrambled, about 3-5 minutes. Place the eggs on a plate and set them aside.
3. Remove the pan from the heat and coat it again with cooking spray and place it over medium-high heat.
4. Add the chicken and carrots and sauté for about 5 minutes or until the chicken is golden brown. Check that the chicken is cooked through before adding the other ingredients.
5. When the chicken is ready, add the chopped scallions, minced garlic, peas, cooked brown rice, the egg whites, and soy sauce. Stir until the ingredients have combined well and continue cooking until all the ingredients are well heated.
6. Serve and enjoy.

Nutritional Information:

Calories 178, Total Fat 2.0 g, Saturated Fat 0.8 g, Total Carbohydrate 21.0 g, Dietary Fiber 38.0 g, Sugars 2.0 g, Protein 18.0 g

4PTS PRESSURE COOK CHICKEN SALAD

Serves: 4, 4 Smart Points™

Ingredients:
2 ½ cups chicken, cooked and chopped
3 stalks celery, chopped
1 cup apple, chopped
¼ cup cranberries, dried
½ cup plain Greek yogurt (nonfat)
2 tablespoons Hellman's mayonnaise, light
2 teaspoons lemon juice
Salt and pepper to taste
Optional:
2 tablespoons fresh parsley, chopped

Directions:
1. In a large bowl, mix the chicken, celery, apple, and dried cranberries. Stir the ingredients and combine them well.
2. In a small bowl, mix the yogurt, mayonnaise, and lemon juice. Add the mixture to the chicken mixture and mix well. Stir in the chopped parsley, if using. Add salt and pepper to taste.
3. Serve on whole grain crackers, rice, pita bread, or make a wrap.

Nutritional Information:
Calories 220 Total Fat 5.0 g, Saturated Fat 1.1 g, Total Carbohydrate 13.0 g, Dietary Fiber 2.0 g, Sugars 7.1 g, Protein 28.0 g

5PTS RASPBERRY BALSAMIC CHICKEN

Serves: 3
5 Smart Points™

Ingredients:
3 pieces boneless skinless chicken breast
¼ cup all-purpose flour
Cooking spray
⅔ Cup chicken broth (low fat)
½ cup raspberry preserve (low sugar)
1 ½ teaspoons cornstarch
1 ½ tablespoons balsamic vinegar
Salt and black pepper to taste

Directions:

1. Cut the boneless and skinless chicken breast into bite-sized pieces. (You may also pound them into thin cutlets to cook through easily.) Season the chicken with salt and black pepper to taste. Dredge the chicken pieces in the flour, and shake off any excess.
2. Heat a non-stick skillet over medium heat and coat it with spray. Cook the chicken for about 15 minutes, turning halfway through so both sides can cook well. Remove the cooked chicken from the skillet.
3. Mix the chicken broth, raspberry preserves, and cornstarch in the skillet over medium heat. Stir in the balsamic vinegar. Add chicken back to the pan. Cook for about 10 minutes, turning halfway through.

Nutritional Information:
Calories 229, Total Fat 4. 6 g, Saturated Fat 0.8 g, Total Carbohydrate 21.8 g, Dietary Fiber 0.7 g, Sugars 15.0 g, Protein 24.5 g

7PTS INSTANT POT VEGETABLE DUCK

Ingredients
- Duck (small size)
- Sliced cucumber half
- Sliced carrots 1
- Cooking wine 7g
- Water 250g
- 1-inch ginger piece
- Salt 10g

Preparation Method
1. Put all ingredients into the instant cooker pot and then press the stew option. Within a few minutes, the delicious soup will be ready in no time.

Nutritional Information
- Preparation Time: 40 minutes
- Total Servings: 2
- Calories: 199
- Calories from Fat: 64
- Fat: 2.9g
- Saturated Fat: 0.9g
- Cholesterol: 55mg
- Carbohydrates: 29.3g
- Fiber: 4.1g
- Sugar: 2.7g
- Protein: 19.3g

PORK, VEAL AND LAMB

5PTS SPICED PORK WITH APPLES

Serves: 6, 5 Smart Points™

Ingredients:
2 (14 ounce) pork tenderloins
Olive oil cooking spray
2 teaspoon 5-spice powder, divided
2 apples, cored and sliced
1 red onion, sliced

Directions:
1. Preheat the oven to 450°F. Remove any excess fat from the pork.
2. Line the baking pan with foil. Spray the foil lightly with olive oil cooking spray. Sprinkle 1 teaspoon 5-spice powder on the pork tenderloins and then place them on the baking pan. Roast the pork for about 20 to 30 minutes, or until it is ready.
3. Meanwhile, spray a non-stick pan with cooking spray and sauté the sliced onion until tender. Add 1 teaspoon 5-spice powder and mix well. Add the apple slices and sauté again until the mixture becomes soft and the onions are cooked. Cut the pork tenderloins into ½-inch slices and top them with the apple and onion mixture. Serve.

Nutritional Information:
Calories 253, Total Fat 9.3 g, Saturated Fat 3.2 g, Total Carbohydrate 9.2 g, Dietary Fiber 1.7 g, Sugars 4.1 g, Protein 31.9 g

4PTS PORK CHOPS WITH SALSA

Serves: 4, 4 Smart Points™

Ingredients:

4 ounces boneless pork loin chops (lean), trimmed
Cooking spray
⅓ Cup salsa
2 tablespoons lime juice, freshly squeezed
¼ cup fresh cilantro or parsley, chopped

Directions:

1. Place the chops on a flat surface and press each one of them with the palm of your hand to flatten them slightly.
2. Coat a large, nonstick skillet with cooking spray. Place it over high heat until the oil becomes hot. Add the chops to the skillet and cook each side for 1 minute, or until they are colored medium-brown. Reduce the heat to medium-low.
3. Mix the salsa and the fresh lime juice together and pour the mixture over the chops. Simmer, uncovered for about 8 minutes or until the chops are cooked through.
4. Garnish the chops with chopped cilantro or parsley, Serve.

Nutritional Information:

Calories 184, Total Fat 8.0 g, Saturated Fat 12.0 g, Total Carbohydrate 2.0 g, Sugars 0.6 g, Protein 25.0 g

7PTS BALSAMIC PORK TENDERLOIN WITH ROASTED BROCCOLI RABE

Serves 4, 7 Smart Points™

Ingredients

1 pork tenderloin, about 1 pound
Salt and freshly ground black pepper
2 bunches broccoli rabe (about 1 pound), trimmed
Cooking spray
2 tablespoons olive oil, divided
2 tablespoons balsamic vinegar

Directions

1. Preheat oven to the broil setting and set oven rack to the upper-middle position. Line a baking sheet with parchment paper and lightly spray with cooking spray.
2. Trim the pork tenderloin from all visible fat and cut into 8 even slices. Season with salt and pepper on both sides.
3. Place broccoli rabe on the baking sheet. Spray lightly with cooking spray. Place in the oven under the broiler for 6-10 minutes until tender and golden brown. Turn the broccoli rabe over halfway through the cooking, about 4-5 minutes.
4. Warm 1 tablespoon of olive oil in a large heavy bottomed sauté pan like a cast iron over medium-high heat. Fry the pork for 8-10 minutes, turning halfway or until cooked your preferred doneness. Take the pan off the heat and remove the pork to a serving plate. Cover lightly with foil to keep warm.
5. Deglaze the pan with the balsamic vinegar and remaining 1 tablespoon of olive oil. Whisk the bottom of the pan to release the browned bits of flavors into the sauce. Season to taste with salt and pepper.
6. To serve, place 2 slices of the pork tenderloin with a quarter of the broccoli rabe on a serving plate. Pour a quarter of the sauce over the meat and vegetables and serve.

Nutritional Information:

Calories 317, Total Fat 16.1 g, Saturated Fat 3.3 g, Total Carbohydrate 3.8 g, Dietary Fiber 2.8 g, Sugars 0 g, Protein 36.2 g

5PTS REAL EASY PORK PICCATA

Serves: 4, 5 Smart Points™

Ingredients:
1 pound pork medallions
1 tablespoon olive oil or cooking spray
½ teaspoon salt
1 teaspoon black pepper
2 cloves garlic, crushed and minced
2 tablespoon capers
¼ cup dry vermouth
¼ cup fresh lemon juice
1 tablespoon fresh chives for garnish (optional)

Directions:
1. Heat the olive oil or cooking spray in a skillet over medium heat.
2. Arrange the pork medallions in the skillet and season with salt and black pepper. Cook for 2-3 minutes per side, or until cooked through.
3. Remove the pork medallions from the heat and keep warm until ready to serve.
4. Add the garlic and capers to the skillet. Cook for 1 minute, stirring gently.
5. Add the vermouth and lemon juice. Continue to cook while stirring and scraping the pan for 1-2 minutes.
6. Remove the sauce from the heat and immediately pour it over the pork medallions for serving.
7. Serve garnished with fresh chives, if desired.

Nutritional Information:
Calories 252, Total Fat 9.4 g, Saturated Fat 2.4 g, Total Carbohydrate 0.2 g, Dietary Fiber 0.1 g, Sugars 0.0 g, Protein 33.4 g

5PTS SLOW COOKER SPICED PULLED PORK

Serves 6

5 Smart Points™

Ingredients

<u>Rub</u>

1 tablespoon paprika

1-3 teaspoons ancho chili powder according to taste

1 teaspoon salt

1 teaspoon ground cumin

1 teaspoon dry oregano

½ teaspoon black pepper

¼ teaspoon cinnamon

¼ teaspoon dry coriander

<u>Other ingredients</u>

2 pounds pork tenderloin, trimmed

1 onion, diced

4 garlic cloves, minced

1 cup low fat beef broth

1 tablespoon apple cider vinegar

Directions

1. Mix together all the rub ingredients in a small bowl.
2. Rub the spice mix all over the pork
3. Place the garlic, onion, and beef broth and apple cider vinegar in the slow cooker. Stir a few times to mix well.
4. Add the pork.
5. Set on LOW and cook for 4-6 hours until the pork is cooked through and shred easily with a fork.

Note: pork can be used to make tacos, sandwiches, and salads.

Nutritional Information:

Calories 190, Total Fat 4.3 g, Saturated Fat 1.2 g, Total Carbohydrate 5.4 g, Dietary Fiber 1.1 g, Sugars 0.9 g, Protein 32.8 g

9PTS HEALTHY CURRIED PORK CHOPS

Serves: 4

9 Smart Points™

Ingredients:

1 pound boneless pork chops, approximately ¼ inch thick

Cooking spray

1 teaspoon salt

1 teaspoon black pepper

2 ½ cups carrots, sliced

1 cup unsweetened coconut milk

1 ½ tablespoon curry powder

1 teaspoon lime zest

Cooked rice for serving, optional

Directions:

1. Preheat the oven to 450°F and spray an 8x8 or larger baking dish with cooking spray.
2. Season the pork with salt and black pepper.
3. Place the pork and the sliced carrots in the baking dish, spreading them out into as even a layer as possible.
4. In a bowl, combine the coconut milk, curry powder, and lime zest. Mix well and pour over the pork.
5. Place the baking dish in the oven and bake for 25-30 minutes, or until the pork is cooked through and the carrots are tender.
6. Remove from the oven and let it rest for several minutes before serving.
7. Serve with cooked rice, if desired.

Nutritional Information:

Calories 367, Total Fat 20.1 g, Saturated Fat 7.5 g, Total Carbohydrate 9.9 g, Dietary Fiber 2.2 g, Sugars 3.4 g, Protein 34.9 g

8PTS SPICY PINEAPPLE PORK

Serves: 4

8 Smart Points™

Ingredients:

1 pound cooked pork, shredded

1 tablespoon vegetable oil or cooking spray

3 cups broccoli florets

1 teaspoon salt

1 teaspoon black pepper

2 cups medium heat tomato salsa, fresh or jarred

2 cups fresh pineapple chunks

¼ cup fresh orange juice (or other citrus juice of choice)

Fresh cilantro for serving (optional)

Cooked rice for serving (optional)

Directions:

1. Heat the vegetable oil or cooking spray in a large skillet over medium heat.
2. Add the broccoli and sauté for 5-7 minutes, or until crisp tender.
3. Add the shredded pork to the skillet and season with salt and black pepper.
4. Next, add the salsa, pineapple chunks, and orange juice. Mix well.
5. Increase the heat to medium high until the liquid comes to a low boil.
6. Reduce the heat to low, cover, and simmer for 5-7 minutes, or until heated through.
7. Remove from the heat and serve with cooked rice and cilantro, if desired.

Nutritional Information:

Calories 328, Total Fat 10.3 g, Saturated Fat 2.5 g, Total Carbohydrate 22.7 g, Dietary Fiber 5.0 g, Sugars 9.4 g, Protein 37.4 g

6PTS BREADED VEAL CUTLETS

Serves 4

6 Smart Points™

Ingredients

1 pound veal cutlets, trimmed

Cooking spray

1/2 cup dry whole-wheat breadcrumbs

1/2 teaspoon paprika

1/2 teaspoon onion powder

1/2 teaspoon salt and black pepper

4 teaspoons canola oil

1 large egg white

4 teaspoons cornstarch

Directions

1. Pound the veal cutlet if needed, so they are ½ inch thick.
2. Preheat oven to 400°F. And line a rimmed baking sheet with parchment paper. Spray lightly with cooking spray.
3. Mix breadcrumbs, and spices in a shallow bowl. Add the oil and mix well.
4. Sprinkle cornstarch over the veal cutlets to evenly coat both sides.
5. Beat the egg white until it becomes frothy. Place in a shallow dish.
6. Add the veal cutlets to the egg white. Massage to coat. Add the cutlets one by one to the breadcrumbs and spices mixt. Try to coat as evenly as possible.
7. Arrange the veal cutlets on the baking sheet. Bake in the preheated oven for 15to 18 minutes, until golden and cooked through.

Nutritional Information:

Calories 219, Total Fat 7 g, Saturated Fat 2.7 g, Total Carbohydrate 11.2 g, Dietary Fiber 1.1 g, Sugars 1.7 g, Protein 24.8 g

5PTS PECAN LEMONY VEAL CUTLETS

Serves 4, 5 Smart Points™

Ingredients

- 4 veal cutlets, about 1 pound of veal
- 1 tablespoon pecans
- 2 tablespoons all-purpose flour
- ¼ teaspoon each salt and black pepper
- ¼ onion powder
- Cooking spray
- 2 teaspoons reduced fat butter spread
- 1 garlic clove, minced
- 1 small French shallot, diced finely
- 1/3 fat-free chicken broth
- 3 tablespoons lemon juice
- 1 teaspoon dry parsley

Directions

1. Pound the veal cutlets if needed so the thickness is ¼ inch thick.
2. In a small food processor, pulse the pecan until almost powder.
3. Mix the flour with the salt, pepper and onion powder. Add the pecan powder.
4. Dredge the veal cutlets in the flour mix on both side.
5. Warm a large heavy skillet such as a cast iron over medium-high heat. Spray lightly the skillet with cooking spray. Fry the veal cutlet for 2-3 minutes on each side, or until golden brown and cooked through. Remove the veal and set aside.
6. Melt the reduced fat butter in the same skillet over medium heat. Add the garlic and shallot and sauté for 1-2 minutes until tender and fragrant.
7. Add the chicken broth, lemon juice and vinegar. With wooden spoon, detach all the browned bits of flavor at the bottom of the pan. Increase the heat to high and bring to a quick boil. Reduce heat to low. Add the veal cutlet and parsley back in the skillet for 2-3 minutes.
8. Serve warm with the sauce.

Nutritional Information:

Calories 224, Total Fat 7.7 g, Saturated Fat 2.2 g, Total Carbohydrate 4.8 g, Dietary Fiber 0.3 g, Sugars 0.2 g, Protein 32.8 g

7PTS LAMB SKEWERS WITH COOL MINT SAUCE

Serves: 4, 7 Smart Points™

Ingredients:

¼ cup soy sauce

2 tablespoons honey

1 pound boneless lamb leg cut into strips

1 cup low fat plain Greek yogurt

½ cup fresh mint leaves, chopped

Salt and freshly ground black pepper, to taste

2 teaspoons five spice powder

½ teaspoon coriander

Bamboo or metal skewers (if using bamboo, soak them in water for 20 minutes before using)

Directions:

1. Preheat an indoor grill over medium heat.
2. Combine the soy sauce and honey together in a bowl. Whisk until blended.
3. Slide each piece of meat onto a metal or bamboo skewer, stretching the strip of lamb out so that it is not bunched together on the skewer.
4. Brush the lamb liberally with the soy sauce mixture. Let set for 10 minutes.
5. Combine the yogurt and mint leaves together Season with salt and pepper to taste. Mix well and place in the refrigerator until ready to serve.
6. Season the meat skewers with salt, black pepper, five spice powder, and coriander. Place the skewers on the grill and cook, turning at least once, for 7-10 minutes, or until the meat has reached the desired doneness.
7. Remove from the heat and serve with cool mint sauce.

Nutritional Information:

Calories 243, Total Fat 8.4 g, Saturated Fat 3.6 g, Total Carbohydrate 14.6 g, Dietary Fiber 1.1 g, Sugars 12.3 g, Protein 26.8 g

6PTS GARLIC INFUSED ROASTED LEG OF LAMB

Serves 8, 6 Smart Points™

Ingredients

3 bulbs of garlic

1 tablespoon lemon zest

2 tablespoons fresh thyme, chopped

3 teaspoons olive oil, divided

Teaspoon each of salt and black pepper, or to taste

3 ½ pounds boneless leg of lamb, trimmed and tied in a roast

Directions

1. Preheat the oven to 350°F. Line a roasting pan with parchment paper or foil.
2. Mince 4 cloves of garlic from one of the bulbs. Mix in a small bowl the minced garlic, lemon zest, 2 ½ teaspoons of olive oil, thyme, and salt and pepper.
3. Rub the meat with the garlic mixture.
4. Cut the top of the garlic bulbs, about ½-inch. Brush the remaining oil on the cut surface of each the garlic bulb.
5. Put the prepared lamb roast in the roasting pan with the garlic bulbs. Insert a meat thermometer in the center of roast and set to 140°F for medium-rare. Place in the oven and roast for about 80-85 minutes, or until the lamb is done to your preferred doneness.
6. When done, remove the lamb from the oven and let rest at least 10 minutes before carving.
7. To serve, place 2 slices of lamb of approximately ¼-inch thick on serving plates. If desired, squish a little of the garlic bulbs directly over the lamb with some of the pan juices (skim the fat first).
8. Serve with your favorite steamed vegetables.

Nutritional Information:

Calories 298, Total Fat 12.1 g, Saturated Fat 4.4 g, Total Carbohydrate 0.3 g, Dietary Fiber 0.2 g, Sugars 0 g, Protein 40.6 g

BEEF RCIPES

8PTS SLOW COOKED FULL OF FLAVOR BEEF CHILI

Serves 8

8 Smart Points™

Ingredients
Cooking spray
1 onion, diced
1 pound extra-lean ground beef
¾ cup diced celery
¾ cup diced green bell pepper
2 garlic cloves, minced
1 teaspoon red chili flakes
2 tablespoons chili powder
2 teaspoons ground cumin
1 teaspoon dry oregano
1 teaspoon dry basil
½ teaspoon each of salt and black pepper
2 (15-ounces) can of kidney beans
2 (10.75-ounces) cans of fire-roasted crushed tomatoes

Directions

1. Coat lightly a large skillet with cooking spray. Brown onion in a skillet over medium heat for 1-2 minutes until tender. Add beef and brown until the meat is cooked. Remove from heat and drain excess fat.
2. Place all the ingredients in the slow cooker. Set on LOW. Cover and let cook for 8 hours.

Nutritional Information:
Calories 273, Total Fat 7.6 g, Saturated Fat 2.7 g, Total Carbohydrate 33.4 g, Dietary Fiber 10.9 g, Sugars 4.9 g, Protein 18.9 g

8PTS SKILLET TERIYAKI BEEF

Serves: 4

8 Smart Points™

Ingredients:
¼ cup soy sauce
¼ cup local honey
1 tablespoon freshly grated ginger
1 pound lean beef steak, thinly sliced
2 teaspoons sesame oil
4 cups fresh snow peas, trimmed
1 teaspoon salt
1 teaspoon black pepper
Cooked rice for serving (optional)
Scallions, sliced for garnish (optional)

Directions:
1. Combine the soy sauce, honey and ginger in a bowl. Whisk together until blended.
2. Place the sliced beef in a bowl and pour the marinade over the meat. Let it set for 15 minutes.
3. Heat the sesame oil in a large skillet over medium.
4. Add the snow peas and sauté for 2-3 minutes.
5. Add the sliced beef, along with the remaining marinade, and season with salt and black pepper.
6. Cook for approximately 7-10 minutes, or until the meat has reached the desired doneness.
7. Remove from the heat and serve immediately with cooked rice, if desired.
8. Garnish with sliced scallions (optional).

Nutritional Information:
Calories 275, Total Fat 10.9 g, Saturated Fat 4.0 g, Total Carbohydrate 18.9 g, Dietary Fiber 2.1 g, Sugars 12.1 g, Protein 25.8 g

7PTS BEEF WITH HERBS RECIPE

Different types of herbs in this recipe are all you need to awake your taste buds again!

Prep time: 5 minutes
Cooking time: 15 minutes
Servings: 3
Ingredients:

- Olive oil – 3 tbsp.
- Onion (chopped) – 1 tbsp.
- Garlic (chopped) – 1 clove
- Thyme (dried) – 1 tsp.
- Rosemary (dried) – ½ tsp.
- Sage (powder) – ¼ tsp.
- Marjoram (dried) – ¼ tsp.
- Salt and pepper to taste
- Hot pepper sauce – 1/8 tsp.
- Beef Steak – 4 pieces
- Parsley – 1 ½ tbsp.

Directions:

1. Get a bowl and add onion, garlic, thyme, sage, marjoram, rosemary, salt and pepper with hot pepper sauce. Mix well.
2. Add beef steak to the instant pot by pouring the mixture over it. Let it cook for 15 minutes on high pressure.
3. When done, Serve with parsley and serve!

Nutrition:

- Calories: 100g
- Fat: 10g
- Carbohydrates: 8g
- Protein: 110g

6PTS BEEF BREAST PIECES WITH CELERY

You will love the chunks of beef in this recipe along with celery!

Prep time: 4 minutes
Cooking time: 25 minutes
Servings: 2
Ingredients:

- Butter – 2 tbsp.
- Onion (chopped) – 1 cup
- Celery (chopped) – 1 cup
- Beef broth (can) – 1
- Beef breast piece (chunks) – 2 lb.
- Vegetable broth (can) – 1
- Carrots – 2 cups sliced
- Basil – 1 tsp.
- Oregano – 1 tsp.
- Salt and pepper according to taste

Directions:

1. Add butter to the instant pot and let it sauté.
2. Add beef broth with celery, onion, vegetable broth, carrots, basil and oregano in it.
3. Let it cook for 5 minutes. Add salt and pepper along with beef pieces. Cook for another 20 minutes.
4. When done, serve and enjoy the meal!

Nutrition:

- Calories:100
- Fat: 6g
- Carbohydrates: 10g
- Protein: 20g

8PTS BEEF WITH POTATO INSTANT POT RECIPE

Prep time: 6 minutes
Cooking time: 20 minutes
Servings: 2
Ingredients:

- Beef Steak pieces – 4 large
- Potatoes – 10 medium size
- Carrots (baby) – 8 ounce
- Celery (chopped) – 1 cup
- Beef soup cans – 2
- Chicken bouillon – 6 cubes
- Garlic salt – 2 tsp.
- Celery salt – 1 tsp.
- Black pepper to taste
- Mixed vegetables (frozen) – 1 small bag

Directions:

1. Get a bowl and mix beef soup with chicken bouillon. Add garlic salt, celery salt, black pepper and mix well.
2. Place the steaks and potatoes in the instant pot and pour the mixture made in step 1 on it. Add carrots, celery, and mixed vegetables on it.
3. Let it cook for 20 minutes.
4. When done, serve and enjoy!

Nutrition:

- Calories: 90
- Fat: 10g
- Carbohydrates: 21g
- Protein: 95g

6PTS BEEF STEAK WITH TOMATO SOUP

Prep time: 4 minutes
Cooking time: 20 minutes
Servings: 2
Ingredients:
- Beef steaks - 4
- Butter – 1 tsp.
- Broth of Beef – 14 ounce
- Tomato soup – 10.74 ounce
- Water – 1 ½ cup
- Cabbage (shredded) – 3 cups
- Onion (chopped) – 1
- Green Bell pepper (diced) – ½ cup
- Salt and pepper to taste

Directions:
1. Add butter to the instant pot. Mix beef broth and tomato soup in the pot. Let it cook for 5 minutes.
2. Now add water with cabbage, onion, bell pepper and salt and pepper. Add beef steaks in it and let it cook for 15 minutes.
3. When the pot beeps, release the pressure and serve!

Nutrition:
- Calories: 90
- Fat: 8g
- Carbohydrates: 20g
- Protein: 25g

5PTS BEEF WITH MUSHROOMS POT RECIPE

Prep time: 6 minutes
Cooking time: 15 minutes
Servings: 2
Ingredients:

- Oil – ¼ cup
- Flour (all-purpose)- ¼ cup
- Bell pepper – 1
- Onion (chopped)- 1
- Beef (chopped, breast) – 2 cups
- Mushrooms- 4.5 ounce
- Tomatoes – diced, 4.5 ounce
- Sauce (any) – 2 tsp.
- Garlic cloves – 3
- Soy sauce – 1 tsp.
- Sugar (white) - 1 tsp.
- Salt and pepper to taste
- Hot sauce – 3 drops

Directions:

1. Get a bowl and add flour, any sauce, soy sauce, sugar, salt and pepper with hot sauce. Mix well.
2. Add oil in the instant pot and place the beef in it. Sprinkle the bell pepper, onion, tomatoes, mushrooms and garlic on it. Pour the mixture and let it cook for 15 minutes.
3. When the pot beeps, take it out and serve!

Nutrition:

- Calories: 155
- Fat: 7g
- Carbohydrates: 10g
- Protein: 40g

6PTS SIMPLE BEEF RECIPE

Prep time: 4 minutes
Cooking time: 20 minutes
Servings: 3
Ingredients:
- Beef breast - 2
- Lemon - 1
- Salt and pepper to taste
- Oil - 1 tbsp.
- Oregano - 1 pinch
- Parsley – 1 cup

Directions:
1. Get a bowl and add lemon, salt, and pepper, oregano, and parsley in it. Mix well.
2. Add oil to the instant pot and place the beef breast in it. Pour the mixture and let it cook for 20 minutes. When done, serve and enjoy!

Nutrition:
- Calories: 100g
- Fat: 10g
- Carbohydrates: 8g
- Protein: 110g

9PTS GRILLED STEAK AND SWEET POTATOES SKEWERS

Serves 4, 9 Smart Points™

Ingredients:

- 3 cups sweet potatoes, cubed
- ½ teaspoon chili powder
- 2 tablespoons rice vinegar
- ¾ cup fresh cilantro, chopped
- ¼ cup low fat sour cream
- 2 cloves garlic, crushed and minced
- 1 teaspoon cumin
- 1 teaspoon lime juice
- 1 pound beef steak, cut into cubes
- 2 cups red bell pepper, chopped into large pieces
- 1 large onion, chopped into large pieces
- 1 tablespoon olive oil, divided
- 1 teaspoon ground black pepper
- ½ teaspoon oregano

Directions

1. Prepare a stovetop grill and preheat the oven to 425°F.
2. On a baking sheet lined with parchment paper, toss together the sweet potatoes, chili powder and enough of the olive oil to lightly coat. Place the baking sheet in the oven and bake while preparing the rest of the ingredients, until the potatoes are firm tender. Remove from the oven and let cool slightly before handling.
3. In a small bowl, combine the rice vinegar, cilantro, sour cream, garlic, cumin, and lime juice. Mix well and set aside.
4. Using wooden or metal skewers, place the steak, sweet potatoes, red bell pepper and onion onto each skewer in an alternating pattern until all ingredients are used.
5. Brush lightly with the remaining vegetable oil, and sprinkle black pepper and oregano.
6. Place the skewers onto the stove top grill and cook, turning once, until steak reaches desired doneness, approximately 5-8 minutes per side.
7. Remove from heat and serve with cilantro sauce.

Nutritional Information:

Calories 319, Total Fat 10.9 g, Saturated Fat 4.6 g, Total Carbohydrate 30.5 g, Dietary Fiber 4.5 g, Sugars 1.6 g, Protein 25.9 g

7PTS EASTERN ISLAND BEEF STEW

Serves 4, 7 Smart Points™

Ingredients:

1 ½ pounds lean beef stew cut into cubes
1 ½ tablespoons flour
1 tablespoon black peppercorns
1 teaspoon five spice powder
4 cloves garlic, crushed and minced
1 tablespoon fresh lemongrass, chopped
2 tablespoons rice vinegar
½ tablespoon low sodium soy sauce
1 tablespoon honey
2 tablespoons olive oil

1 cup red onion, chopped
2 cups carrots, chopped
½ cup poblano pepper, diced
1 tablespoon jalapeno pepper
4 cups tomatoes, chopped
2 tablespoons tomato paste
2 cups acorn squash, cubed
3 cups low sodium beef broth
1 cinnamon stick
2 cardamom pods
2 star anise pods

Directions:

1. In a bowl, combine the flour, peppercorns, and five spice powder. Toss the stew meat in the flour mixture, coating generously.
2. Mix in the garlic, lemongrass, rice vinegar, soy sauce, and honey. Mix well and refrigerate for at least 30 minutes.
3. Preheat the oven to 325°F.
4. Add the olive oil to a Dutch oven over medium heat. Add the beef, onions, and carrots. Sauté until meat is lightly browned, approximately 3-5 minutes.
5. Add the poblano and jalapeno peppers, and cook for 1-2 minutes.
6. Add the tomatoes, tomato paste, squash, beef stock, cinnamon stick, cardamom and star anise. Continue to cook, while stirring until well blended, approximately 3-5 minutes.
7. Cover the Dutch oven and place in the oven to bake for approximately 40 minutes, or until the meat is cooked through and tender.

Nutritional Information:

Calories 231, Total Fat 7.7 g, Saturated Fat 2.7 g, Total Carbohydrate 22.8 g, Dietary Fiber 4.2 g, Sugars 6.2 g, Protein 19.6 g

6PTS GROUND BEEF WITH SPINACH LEAVES

Want to fill your stomach today? Here is a full stomach recipe for you!
Prep time: 6 minutes
Cooking time: 19 minutes
Servings: 2
Ingredients:
- Ground beef – 1 lb.
- Onion (chopped) – 1
- Garlic (minced) – 2 cloves
- Tomato sauce – 2 cups
- Worcestershire sauce – 1 tbsp.
- Beef broth – 2 cups
- Tomatoes - 2 diced
- Spinach leaves – ½ bunch chopped
- Salt and pepper to taste
- Cheese to Serve

Directions:
1. Add beef broth in the instant pot. Let it boil for 2 minutes. Add onion, garlic, tomato sauce, Worcestershire sauce and tomatoes in it.
2. Add beef and let it cook for 15 minutes. Add spinach leaves with salt and pepper to it. Cook it for 2 more minutes. When ready, serve with sprinkling cheese over it!

Nutrition:
- Calories: 155
- Fat: 7g
- Carbohydrates: 10g
- Protein: 40g

6PTS
BEEF WITH BEANS RECIPE

A great combination of beans and beef is the best one which you can learn and try today with your family for dinner!

Prep time: *5 minutes*
Cooking time: *10 minutes*
Servings: *4*
Ingredients:

- Beans – 2 cups
- Beef stock – 2 cups
- Grounded beef – 4 cups
- Yellow mustard – 2 cups
- Onion (minced) – 1
- Chili powder – ½ tbsp.
- Cumin powder – 1 tbsp.
- White vinegar – 1 tbsp.
- Salt and pepper to taste

Directions:

1. Add beef stock, yellow mustard, onion, chili powder and salt and pepper in the instant pot. Let it sauté.
2. Add grounded beef in it with beans and cumin powder. Mix well. Let it cook for 10 minutes.
3. When ready, serve and enjoy!

Nutrition:

- Calories: 90
- Fat: 10g
- Carbohydrates: 21g
- Protein: 95g

8PTS BEEF STEAK WITH MUSTARD

Mustard is a great addition to enjoy the food and to make it even more delicious so try this recipe now!

Prep time: *4 minutes*
Cooking time: *15 minutes*
Servings: *3*
Ingredients:

- Soy sauce – ½ cup
- Wine vinegar – ¼ cup
- Sugar (brown) – ¼ cup
- Green onions (sliced) – ¼ cup
- Garlic (chopped) – 1 tbsp.
- Mustard powder – 1 tbsp.
- Beef Steak – 2 pounds
- Sesame seeds – 2 tbsp.

Directions:

1. Get a bowl and mix soy sauce, wine vinegar, sugar, mustard powder and sesame seeds in it. Mix well.
2. Add this mixture to the instant pot with beef steaks. Sprinkle the green onions with chopped garlic. Let it cook for 15 minutes.
3. When ready, serve!

Nutrition:

- Calories: 100
- Fat: 20g
- Carbohydrates: 8g
- Protein: 60g

7PTS BEEF WORCESTERSHIRE RECIPE

A great sauce to make the food even more delicious to eat all weekend!
Prep time: *4 minutes*
Cooking time: *20 minutes*
Servings: *2*
Ingredients:

- *Balsamic Vinegar – ½ cup*
- *Soy sauce – ¼ cup*
- *Garlic (chopped) – 3 tbsp.*
- *Honey – 2 tbsp.*
- *Olive oil – 2 tbsp.*
- *Salt and pepper to taste*
- *Worcestershire sauce – 1 tsp.*
- *Onion powder – 1 tsp.*
- *Smoke flavor liquid – 1 tsp.*
- *Cayenne pepper – 1 pinch*
- *Beef Steaks – 2 (½ pound)*

Directions:

1. *Get a bowl and add balsamic vinegar, soy sauce, honey, salt and pepper, garlic, Worcestershire sauce, onion powder and cayenne powder. Stir well.*
2. *Add the beef steak to the instant pot and pour the mixture over it. Add olive oil and let it cook for 20 minutes.*
3. *When ready, take it out and serve!*

Nutrition:

- *Calories: 100*
- *Fat: 20g*
- *Carbohydrates: 8g*
- *Protein: 60g*

8PTS MAPLE SYRUP MIX BEEF RECIPE

Maple syrup can be used in any recipe. Check it out here!

Prep time: 5 minutes
Cooking time: 15 minutes
Servings: 2
Ingredients:

- Soy sauce – ½ cup
- Maple syrup – ¼ cup
- Garlic (chopped) – 6 cloves
- Ginger (grated) – 1 tbsp.
- Mustard powder – 1 tsp.
- Sesame oil – 1 tsp.
- Hot pepper sauce – ¼ tsp.
- Beer – ½ cup
- Beef steak – 4 (10 ounce)

Directions:

1. Mix soy sauce, garlic, ginger, mustard powder, hot pepper sauce, maple syrup and beer together in a bowl.
2. Add sesame oil to the instant pot and place the beef steak on it. Pour the mixture and let it cook for 15 minutes.
3. Serve when ready!

Nutrition:

- Calories: 155
- Fat: 7g
- Carbohydrates: 10g
- Protein: 40g

5PTS CREOLE CRUSTED RIBEYE'S

Serves 4, 5 Smart Points™

Ingredients

4 ribeye steaks, approximately 5 ounces each
¼ cup Dijon mustard
½ teaspoon cayenne sauce
1 tablespoon shallot, chopped
1 tablespoon vegetable oil
½ teaspoon black pepper
½ teaspoon allspice
2 cloves garlic, crushed and minced
2 cups green bell peppers, sliced
1 cup cremini mushrooms, sliced

Directions

1. Preheat oven to 400°F
2. In a bowl, combine the Dijon mustard, cayenne sauce, and shallots. Mix well and set aside.
3. Add the vegetable oil to a large ovenproof skillet over medium high heat.
4. Coat the steaks with the black pepper, allspice, and garlic. Place them in the skillet and sear on both sides, just until browned, approximately 2-3 minutes per side.
5. Remove from the pan and keep warm.
6. Add the bell peppers and mushrooms to the skillet and sauté for 2-3 minutes. Remove from heat.
7. Place the steaks on top of the peppers and mushrooms. Spread the mustard mixture onto each steak, and press some bread crumbs on top.
8. Place in the oven and bake until steak has reached desired doneness, approximately 15 minutes.

Nutritional Information:

Calories 205, Total Fat 8.5 g, Saturated Fat 3.6 g, Total Carbohydrate 5.5 g, Dietary Fiber 1.2 g, Sugars 1.8 g, Protein 24.2 g

5PTS BEEF MEDALLIONS WITH ROSEMARY MUSHROOM SAUCE

Serves: 4

5 Smart Points™

Ingredients:

1 pound beef medallions

1 teaspoon salt

1 teaspoon coarse ground black pepper

1 tablespoon olive oil or cooking spray

2 cups assorted mushrooms, sliced

3 cloves garlic, crushed and minced

¼ cup dry red wine

1 tablespoon fresh rosemary, chopped

Directions:

1. Preheat the broiler and line a baking sheet with aluminum foil.
2. Arrange the medallions on the baking sheet and season with salt and black pepper.
3. Place the medallions under the broiler for 5-7 minutes, turning once, until the desired doneness is reached.
4. Remove from heat and set aside.
5. In the meantime, heat the olive oil or cooking spray in a skillet over medium heat.
6. Add the mushrooms and garlic. Sauté for 3-4 minutes.
7. Add the red wine to the skillet and cook, scraping the pan, for 1-2 minutes.
8. Remove the sauce from the heat and immediately pour it over the beef medallions before serving.

Nutritional Information:

Calories 195, Total Fat 8.6 g, Saturated Fat 3.7 g, Total Carbohydrate 1.5 g, Dietary Fiber 0.4 g, Sugars 0.7 g, Protein 24.1 g

5PTS AUTHENTIC ITALIAN STEAK ROLLS

Serves: 4, 5 Smart Points™

Ingredients:
1 pound flank steak, thinly sliced in sheets
¼ cup low fat Italian salad dressing
1 cup red bell pepper, sliced
½ pound asparagus spears, trimmed
1 cup onion, sliced
Cooking spray
1 teaspoon salt
1 teaspoon black pepper
Kitchen twine

Directions:
1. Place the steaks in a bowl and cover them with the Italian salad dressing. Toss to coat. Set aside for 15 minutes.
2. Preheat the oven to 350°F and line a baking sheet with aluminum foil.
3. Remove the meat from the marinade and lay the slices out on a flat surface. Season with salt and black pepper as desired.
4. Place the red bell pepper, asparagus and onion pieces on the center of each piece of meat in equal amounts.
5. Roll up each piece of meat around the vegetables and secure with kitchen twine.
6. Heat the cooking spray in a skillet over medium high.
7. Add the steak rolls to the skillet and sear on all sides.
8. Transfer the steak rolls to the baking sheet. Place it in the oven and bake for 15-20 minutes, or until the meat is cooked through and the vegetables are crisp tender.
9. Remove from the oven and let rest 5 minutes before serving.

Nutritional Information:
Calories 211, Total Fat 8.6 g, Saturated Fat 3.7 g, Total Carbohydrate 7.9 g, Dietary Fiber 1.9 g, Sugars 1.8 g, Protein 24.6 g

8PTS INSTANT BEEF SOBA BOWLS

Serves: 4, 8 Smart Points™

Ingredients:

1 pound flank or skirt steak, thinly sliced

Cooking spray

1 teaspoon salt

1 teaspoon black pepper

1 teaspoon ground ginger

4 cups fresh snow peas, washed and trimmed

¼ cup soy sauce

1 cup beef stock

½ pound soba noodles, cooked

Fresh cilantro for garnish (optional)

Lime wedges for garnish (optional)

Directions:

1. Spray a large skillet with vegetable oil and heat over medium.
2. Add the steak slices and season with salt, black pepper, and ground ginger. Cook, stirring occasionally, for 5-7 minutes, or until the meat has reached the desired doneness.
3. Remove the steak from the pan and keep it warm.
4. Add the snow peas to the pan and sauté for 2-3 minutes.
5. Combine the beef stock and soy sauce and add them to the skillet. Cook for 2-3 minutes, or until the liquid comes to a low boil.
6. Add the cooked soba noodles and toss. Cook an additional 1-2 minutes, or until warmed through.
7. Transfer the noodles, broth, and snow peas to a serving bowl and top with slices of steak.
8. Garnish with fresh cilantro and lime wedges before serving, if desired.

Nutritional Information:

Calories 328, Total Fat 8.8 g, Saturated Fat 3.7 g, Total Carbohydrate 31.1 g, Dietary Fiber 2.1 g, Sugars 3.5 g, Protein 32.7 g

5PTS TRADITION BEEF ROPE VIEJAS

Serves 6
5 Smart Points™

Ingredients

Cooking spray

2 pounds flank steak, trimmed

2 bell peppers, trimmed and cut into bite sized pieces

1 onion, sliced thinly

4 garlic cloves, minced

1-2 bay leaves

1 teaspoon cumin

1 teaspoon oregano

¼ teaspoon salt

¼ teaspoon black pepper

¾ cup non-fat beef broth

3 tablespoons tomato paste

Directions

1. Lightly spray the slow cooker with cooking spray.
2. Add the beef, peppers, onion, garlic and spices to the slow cooker.
3. Mix the beef broth and the tomato paste in a bowl. Add it to the slow cooker.
4. Set on LOW and slow cook for 8 hours.

Nutritional Information:

Calories 262, Total Fat 10 g, Saturated Fat 3.7 g, Total Carbohydrate 7.2 g, Dietary Fiber 1.1 g, Sugars 2.7 g, Protein 35.8 g

7PTS STEAK WITH LEEK PAN SAUCE

Serves: 4

7 Smart Points™

Ingredients:

4 lean beef steaks, approximately 4-5 ounces each

Cooking spray

1 teaspoon salt

1 teaspoon coarse ground black pepper

½ teaspoon onion powder

½ teaspoon oregano

1 cup leeks, sliced

½ cup dry red wine

1 cup beef stock

¼ cup gorgonzola cheese crumbles

Directions:

1. Heat the cooking spray in a deep skillet over medium-high heat.
2. Season the steaks with salt, black pepper, onion powder and oregano. Place the steaks in the skillet and sear on all sides, then remove and keep warm.
3. Add the leeks to the skillet and sauté for 2-3 minutes.
4. Next, add the red wine and reduce for 2-3 minutes, scraping the bottom of the pan to remove any steak bits.
5. Add the beef stock and return the steaks to the skillet.
6. Bring to a low boil before reducing the heat to medium low and cooking for 7-10 minutes, or until the steaks have reached desired doneness.
7. Remove the skillet from the heat and transfer the steaks to serving plates. Spoon the pan sauce and leeks over the steaks and then garnish with crumbled gorgonzola.
8. Let the steaks rest for 5 minutes before slicing.

Nutritional Information:

Calories 250, Total Fat 10.8 g, Saturated Fat 5.2 g, Total Carbohydrate 5.1 g, Dietary Fiber 0.5 g, Sugars 1.4 g, Protein 26.3 g

6PTS COOL AND TANGY BEEF CUPS

Serves: 4
6 Smart Points™

Ingredients:
1 pound roast beef, cooked and shredded
1 cup carrot, shredded
½ cup scallions, sliced
2 tablespoons rice vinegar
½ teaspoon salt
1 teaspoon black pepper
1 teaspoon crushed red pepper flakes
8 large Bibb lettuce leaves
Fresh mint, chopped for garnish (optional)

Directions:
1. Combine the roast beef, carrots, and scallions in a bowl. Toss to mix.
2. Season the beef with rice vinegar, salt, black pepper, and crushed red pepper flakes. Mix well.
3. Spoon the beef mixture into the center of each leaf.
4. Garnish with fresh mint before serving.

Nutritional Information:
Calories 201, Total Fat 8.5 g, Saturated Fat 3.6 g, Total Carbohydrate 6.2 g, Dietary Fiber 1.2 g, Sugars 4.1 g, Protein 23.6 g

FISH AND SEAFOOD RECIPES

2PTS PONZU POCKETS

Serves: 4

2 Smart Points™

Ingredients:

4 cups fresh spinach, torn

1 cup zucchini, cut into matchsticks

4 flounder fillets, approximately 4-5 ounces each

½ teaspoon salt

1 teaspoon black pepper

½ teaspoon ground ginger

1 tablespoon ponzu sauce

1 teaspoon sesame oil

Directions:

1. Preheat the oven to 450°F.
2. Lay out four pieces of aluminum foil, each measuring approximately 12 inches.
3. Place equal amounts of spinach and zucchini into the center of each piece of foil.
4. Place a flounder fillet over the vegetables and season the fish with salt, black pepper and ground ginger.
5. Drizzle each portion with ponzu sauce and sesame oil.
6. Close each piece of foil over the fish in an envelope style fold.
7. Place the packets in a baking dish and in the oven.
8. Bake for 15 minutes.
9. Remove from the oven and open carefully to allow the steam to escape before serving.

Nutritional Information:

Calories 114, Total Fat 2.3 g, Saturated Fat 0.2 g, Total Carbohydrate 2.9 g, Dietary Fiber 1.3 g, Sugars 0.9 g, Protein 21.1 g

1PTS LEMON DIJON WHITEFISH

Serves: 4
1 Smart Points™

Ingredients:
1 pound whitefish fillets
Cooking spray
2 tablespoons Dijon mustard
1 teaspoon prepared horseradish
1 tablespoon fresh lemon juice
1 teaspoon salt
1 teaspoon black pepper
1 lemon, sliced

Directions:
1. Preheat the oven to 450°F and spray a 9x9 or larger baking dish with cooking spray.
2. In a bowl, combine the Dijon mustard, horseradish, and lemon juice.
3. Brush each whitefish fillet with the Dijon mixture, season with salt and pepper as desired, and then place it in the baking dish.
4. Place the lemon slices over the top of the fish.
5. Place the fish in the oven and bake for 15 minutes, or until the fish is cooked through and flakey.

Nutritional Information:
Calories 99, Total Fat 1.0 g, Saturated Fat 0.0 g, Total Carbohydrate 0.4 g, Dietary Fiber 0.1 g, Sugars 0.3 g, Protein 20.0 g

3PTS CREAMY CUCUMBER SALMON

Serves: 4
3 Smart Points™

Ingredients:
1 pound salmon steaks
½ cup plain low fat Greek yogurt
½ cup cucumber, peeled and finely diced
1 tablespoon fresh dill, chopped
½ teaspoon salt
1 teaspoon black pepper
1 tablespoon olive oil or cooking spray
½ teaspoon ground coriander
1 teaspoon fresh lemon juice

Directions:
1. Prepare a stovetop grill over medium heat.
2. In a bowl combine the low fat Greek yogurt, cucumber, dill and a pinch of the salt and black pepper. Mix well and place in the refrigerator until ready to serve.
3. Brush the salmon steaks with olive oil or spray a light coat of cooking spray. Season the salmon with the remaining salt, black pepper, coriander, and lemon juice.
4. Place the salmon steaks on the grill, and cook 12-15 minutes, depending on thickness, turning once about halfway through, until the salmon is flakey in the center.
5. Remove from the heat and serve with a dollop of cucumber sauce.

Nutritional Information:
Calories 186, Total Fat 5.0 g, Saturated Fat 0.8 g, Total Carbohydrate 2.9 g, Dietary Fiber 0.6 g, Sugars 2.0 g, Protein 30.6 g

4PTS SALMON GLAZED WITH HONEY

Serves: 4

4 Smart Points™

Ingredients:

4 pieces salmon fillet

3 tablespoons rice wine (sweet)

1 tablespoon honey

1 tablespoon rice vinegar, seasoned

1 tablespoon soy sauce

1 teaspoon ginger, minced

¼ cup scallions, thinly sliced

Salt and pepper to taste

Cooking spray

Directions:

1. In a small saucepan, mix the sweet wine, honey, vinegar, soy sauce, and ginger. Bring them to a boil over medium-high heat to make the sauce. Cook the sauce while stirring regularly for about 5 minutes, until it has thickened and the flavors have blended well. Remove it from the heat and then cover it with a lid to keep it warm.
2. In the meantime, sprinkle the salmon with salt and pepper and spray a large nonstick skillet with the vegetable oil spray. Set it over high heat. Add the salmon fillet pieces and cook for about 4 minutes on each side, or until the fish is browned. Turn the fillet once halfway through. Use a spoon to spread the sauce over the fish and sprinkle with the scallions. Serve hot.

Nutritional Information:

Calories 180, Total Fat 5.0 g, Saturated Fat 0.9 g, Total Carbohydrate 5.9 g, Dietary Fiber 0.3 g, Sugars 4.1 g, Protein 23.7 g

3PTS REAL EASY GLAZED SALMON

Serves: 4
3 Smart Points™

Ingredients:
1 pound salmon steaks
Cooking spray
2 tablespoons soy sauce
1 tablespoon rice vinegar
1 tablespoon shallots, diced
½ teaspoon salt
1 teaspoon black pepper
1 tablespoon toasted sesame seeds

Directions:
1. Spray a skillet with the cooking spray and heat it over medium high.
2. In a bowl, combine the soy sauce, rice vinegar and shallots. Whisk until blended.
3. Season the salmon with salt and black pepper and then brush each steak with the glaze.
4. Reduce the heat of the skillet to medium and place the salmon in the pan, skin side down (if the skin is still attached).
5. Cook for 5-7 minutes per side, or until the salmon is cooked through.
6. Remove from the skillet and sprinkle with toasted sesame seeds before serving.

Nutritional Information:
Calories 186, Total Fat 6.1 g, Saturated Fat 1.0 g, Total Carbohydrate 1.1 g, Dietary Fiber 0.3 g, Sugars 0.1 g, Protein 29.9 g

8PTS ANGEL HAIR SHRIMP AND TOMATO PASTA

Serves: 4
8 Smart Points™

Ingredients:
8 ounces angel hair (vermicelli) pasta, cooked
½ cup onion, diced
2 cups heirloom tomatoes, chopped
1 pound shrimp, cleaned and deveined
6 cups fresh spinach, torn
1 tablespoon olive oil
1 teaspoon salt
1 teaspoon black pepper
1 teaspoon crushed red pepper flakes

Directions:
1. Pour the olive oil in a large skillet over medium heat.
2. Place the onion in the skillet and sauté for 2-3 minutes.
3. Add the tomatoes and cook for an additional 2 minutes.
4. Add the shrimp to the skillet, and cook for 5 minutes, stirring frequently. The shrimp should turn pink.
5. Place the spinach in the skillet with the other ingredients and cook until wilted, approximately 1-2 minutes.
6. Add the cooked pasta to the skillet and toss to mix. Reduce the heat to low and cook until the pasta is heated through, approximately 2-4 minutes.
7. Remove from the heat and serve immediately.

Nutritional Information:
Calories 357, Total Fat 3.5 g, Saturated Fat 0.4 g, Total Carbohydrate 50.6 g, Dietary Fiber 4.3 g, Sugars 1.2 g, Protein 32.3 g

5PTS SIMPLE PASTA AND TUNA SALAD

Serves: 6
5 Smart Points™

Ingredients:
6 ounces pasta
1 (12 ounce) can tuna, drained
¼ cup celery, diced
½ cup cherry tomatoes cut in halves
½ cup yellow bell pepper, cut into strips
¾ cup salsa, (low-salt)
½ cup mayonnaise (low-fat)
½ teaspoon red pepper, ground
2 tablespoons scallions, sliced

Directions:
1. Start by cooking the pasta according to the package instructions, but omit the fat and salt.
2. Drain the pasta and rinse it with cold water.
3. In a large bowl, mix together the pasta, tuna, celery, cherry tomatoes, and sliced bell pepper until everything has combined well.
4. In a small bowl, mix together the salsa, mayonnaise, and ground red pepper until they have combined well. Add the dressing to the pasta mixture and toss. Cover and chill. Sprinkle the mixture with scallions and serve.

Nutritional Information:
Calories 194, Total Fat 2.0 g, Saturated Fat 1.0 g, Total Carbohydrate 25.0 g, Dietary Fiber 2.0 g, Sugars 2.0 g, Protein 18.0 g

5PTS SALMON IN GINGER AND SOY

Serves: 6
5 Smart Points™

Ingredients:
6 fillets fresh salmon, skinned
⅓ Cup soy sauce
¼ cup brown sugar
2 garlic cloves, minced
2 teaspoon fresh ginger, minced

Directions:
1. Prepare the marinade in advance by combining soy sauce, brown sugar, ginger, and garlic together in a small bowl. Place the salmon fillets in a large resealable bag and pour in the marinade. Turn the bag to coat the salmon, and refrigerate.
2. Turn the fish from time to time so the marinade can cover it all. In the meantime, preheat the oven to 425°F.
3. Remove the fish from the fridge and seal it in a square of aluminum foil. Place it on a baking sheet and put it in the oven.
4. Cook for 15 minutes, or until the salmon is properly cooked. You'll know it has cooked through when it flakes easily when pressed with a fork. Serve immediately and enjoy.

Nutritional Information:
Calories 192.0, Total Fat 7.0 g, Saturated Fat 1.5 g, Total Carbohydrate 7.0 g, Dietary Fiber 0.0 g, Sugars 3.8 g, Protein 23.0 g

7PTS GRILLED SHRIMP AND WATERMELON SALAD

Serves: 4, 7 Smart Points™

Ingredients:

For the shrimp:

10 ounces large shrimp, shelled and deveined

1 garlic clove, crushed to a paste

Salt to taste (seasoned)

For dressing:

1 tablespoon shallots, chopped

1 teaspoon water

2 ½ tablespoons golden balsamic vinegar

⅛ Teaspoon kosher salt

Pinch of black pepper

2 tablespoons extra-virgin olive oil

For salad:

8 cups romaine, chopped

4 cups watermelon, diced

4 ounces soft goat cheese

Directions:

1. Take a small bowl and mix shallots, water, vinegar, salt, and pepper. Add olive oil little by little stirring until it has combined well. Season the shrimp with seasoned salt, and then add the garlic, mixing it in. You may thread the shrimp onto pre-soaked skewers.
2. Light the grill (or use an indoor grill pan if you are not using skewers) on medium to medium-high heat. Grill each side of the shrimp for about 1 or 2 minutes. Set them aside when ready.
3. In a large bowl, toss the romaine with the dressing. Divide it on 4 plates. Top with watermelon, goat cheese, and the shrimp. Enjoy.

Nutritional Information:

Calories 293, Total Fat 18.0 g, Saturated Fat 8,8 g Total Carbohydrate 12.0 g, Dietary Fiber 2.0 g, Sugars 7.0 g, Protein 22.0 g

7PTS LOW POINTS SHRIMP WITH PASTA

Serves: 1
7 Smart Points™

Ingredients:
¼ cup chopped onions
2 garlic cloves, chopped
1 teaspoon olive oil
2 tablespoons white wine
½ cup cooked shrimp
Fresh parsley, to taste
1 cup whole wheat pasta, cooked
1 tablespoon Parmesan cheese, grated
Black pepper, coarsely ground

Directions:
1. Sauté the onions and garlic in a nonstick skillet with the olive oil.
2. Add the white wine and reduce the heat.
3. Stir in the shrimp and parsley, and cook until the shrimp is warmed through.
4. Add the cooked pasta and stir until all the pasta has been coated. Add the cheese and pepper. Serve and enjoy. You can serve with a green salad to enrich it and make the meal very satisfying.

Nutritional Information:
Calories 415, Total Fat 8.5 g, Saturated Fat 3.7 g Total Carbohydrate 46.7 g, Dietary Fiber 7.2 g, Sugars 18.0 g, Protein 35.1 g

8PTS TASTY BAKED CURRY SCALLOPS

Serves: 4

8 Smart Points™

Ingredients:

1 pound scallops

Cooking spray

1 cup onion, thinly sliced

1 cup red bell pepper, thinly sliced

1 teaspoon salt

1 teaspoon black pepper

1 ½ cups unsweetened coconut milk

1 tablespoon curry powder

Fresh cilantro for garnish (optional)

Cooked rice for serving (optional)

Directions:

1. Preheat the oven to 375°F, and lightly spray an 8x8 or larger baking dish.
2. Place the onion and red bell pepper in the baking dish, followed by the scallops.
3. Season the scallops with salt and black pepper.
4. Combine the coconut milk with the curry powder and pour it over the scallops.
5. Place the baking dish in the oven and bake for 15 minutes, or until the scallops are cooked through.
6. Remove it from the oven and let it rest for 3-5 minutes before serving.
7. Garnish with fresh cilantro and serve with cooked rice, if desired.

Nutritional Information:

Calories 249, Total Fat 16.9 g, Saturated Fat 10.7 g, Total Carbohydrate 10.7 g, Dietary Fiber 1.1 g, Sugars 1.9 g, Protein 25.8 g

3PTS BAKED SHRIMP WITH SPICES

Serves: 4
3 Smart Points™

Ingredients:
Olive oil cooking spray
1 tablespoon honey
2 teaspoons creole seasoning
2 teaspoons parsley, dried
1 teaspoon olive oil
2 tablespoons lemon juice, freshly squeezed
2 teaspoons soy sauce (low-sodium)
1 pound large shrimp, peeled

Directions:
1. Preheat the oven to 450°F. Coat an 11x7 baking dish with the olive oil spray.
2. In the baking dish, combine the honey, creole seasoning, dried parsley, olive oil, lemon juice, and soy sauce and stir well so that all the ingredients have combined well.
3. Add the shrimp to the mixture and toss it to coat.
4. Bake the coated shrimp for about 8 minutes, or until turns pink, but ensure you keep stirring from time to time. Remove from the oven and serve.

Nutritional Information:
Calories 111, Total Fat 2.0 g, Saturated Fat 0.4 g, Total Carbohydrate 6.0 g, Dietary Fiber 0.0 g, Sugars 5.0 g, Protein 16.0 g

4PTS SIMPLE COASTAL TUNA SALAD

Serves: 4
4 Smart Points™

Ingredients:
½ pound tuna, canned or cooked and flaked
1 cup artichoke hearts, quartered
1 cup red bell pepper, chopped
1 cup cherry tomatoes, quartered
1 tablespoon lemon juice
2 tablespoons olive oil
1 teaspoon salt
1 teaspoon black pepper
½ teaspoon oregano
½ cup fresh parsley, chopped (optional)
Leaf lettuce for serving (optional)

Directions:
1. In a bowl, combine the tuna, artichoke hearts, red bell pepper, and tomatoes. Toss to mix.
2. Drizzle the salad with lemon juice and olive oil, then season with salt, black pepper, and oregano. Add the fresh parsley last, and toss gently to mix.
3. Cover and refrigerate for at least 30 minutes before serving.
4. Serve on a bed of leaf lettuce, if desired.

Nutritional Information:
Calories 163, Total Fat 7.8 g, Saturated Fat 1.1 g, Total Carbohydrate 5.0 g, Dietary Fiber 2.1 g, Sugars 0.8 g, Protein 18.0 g

Salads and Soups

6PTS Raspberry Chicken Salad

Serves: 4, 6 Smart Points™

Ingredients:
- 6 cup mixed greens (arugula, endive, spinach, etc.)
- 2 cups cooked chicken, shredded or cubed
- ¼ cup walnuts, chopped
- 1 cup fresh raspberries
- ½ cup feta cheese

Directions:
1. Thoroughly rinse the greens and combine them in a bowl. Toss to mix.
2. Add the chicken and walnuts to the bowl and toss again.
3. At this point, you can either keep all of the ingredients in the large bowl for serving or transfer the salad to individual serving plates.
4. Top the salad with fresh raspberries and crumbled feta cheese.
5. Serve immediately while the greens are still crisp.

Nutritional Information:
Calories 197, Total Fat 10.7 g, Saturated Fat 3.7 g, Total Carbohydrate 5.4 g, Dietary Fiber 4.1 g, Sugars 0.9 g, Protein 17.7 g

5PTS Asparagus and Stilton Chicken Salad

Serves: 4, 5 Smart Points™

Ingredients:
- 1 ½ pounds fresh asparagus, trimmed
- 12 endive leaves, trimmed
- 2 cups chicken, cooked and sliced
- ½ teaspoon salt, optional
- ½ teaspoon black pepper, optional
- ¼ cup stilton cheese crumbles
- ½ lemon, zested and juiced

Directions:
1. Place the asparagus spears in a skillet and add just enough water to cover.
2. Turn the heat on to medium-high and bring the water to a boil. Cover, reduce the heat to low and simmer for approximately 5 minutes, or until the asparagus is firm tender.
3. Remove the asparagus from the pan and immediately place it in a bowl of cold water for 1 minute.
4. Remove the asparagus from the water, drain well and set aside.
5. Arrange 3 endive leaves on each plate, topped with the sliced chicken.
6. Season with salt and pepper, if desired.
7. Next, sprinkle on the stilton cheese crumbles and top with the asparagus.
8. Drizzle with lemon juice to your liking and garnish with lemon zest before serving.

Nutritional Information:
Calories 181, Total Fat 7.0 g, Saturated Fat 4.0 g, Total Carbohydrate 10.4 g, Dietary Fiber 6.8 g, Sugars 0.3 g, Protein 21.0 g

4PTS Chicken and Spinach Crescent Rings

Serves: 8, 4 Smart Points™

Ingredients:
- 5 ounces grilled chicken, cut in strips
- 1 cup baby spinach, fresh
- 1 (8 ounce) can crescent roll dough (reduced fat)
- 4 tablespoons whipped cream cheese (reduced fat), softened
- ⅓ Cup Mexican blend cheese (reduced fat), shredded
- Spices of your choice

Directions:
1. Preheat the oven to 375°F.
2. Arrange the crescent roll dough, unrolled, on an ungreased baking sheet. Spread the cream cheese on each, and then season with your favorite spices.
3. Place the spinach on top of the cream cheese and lay on the grilled chicken strips. Sprinkle with the Mexican blend cheese. Make the rings by pulling the ends of each crescent roll up and wrapping it around the filling. Tuck them so they retain the shape.
4. Bake for 14 minutes, or until the crescent rolls become golden brown.

Nutritional Information:
Calories 142, Total Fat 5.0 g, Saturated Fat 2.0 g, Total Carbohydrate 16.0 g, Dietary Fiber 1.0 g, Sugars 1.0 g, Protein 8.0 g

5PTS Tender Chicken Club Salad

Serves: 4, 5 Smart Points™

Ingredients:
- 8 cups mixed dark salad greens
- 1 pound chicken, cooked and sliced
- ½ cup bacon, cooked and diced
- 2 cups heirloom tomatoes, cut into wedges
- ½ cup fat free ranch dressing

Directions:
1. Place the salad greens in a bowl and add the fat free ranch dressing. Toss to coat.
2. Next, add the chicken, bacon, and tomatoes. Toss to mix.
3. Serve immediately, or cover and refrigerate for up to two hours before serving.

Nutritional Information:

Calories 215, Total Fat 4.6 g, Saturated Fat 1.3 g, Total Carbohydrate 11.0 g, Dietary Fiber 1.3 g, Sugars 5.2 g, Protein 28.1 g

6PTS Roasted Caprese Salad with Chicken

Serves: 4, 6 Smart Points™

Ingredients:
- 4 cups heirloom grape tomatoes, halved
- 1 ½ tablespoons olive oil
- 1 teaspoon salt, divided
- 1 teaspoon black pepper, divided
- 1 pound boneless, skinless chicken breast, cooked and sliced
- 1 cup fresh mozzarella bocconcini
- ½ cup fresh basil, torn
- 1 tablespoon balsamic vinegar

Directions:
1. Preheat the oven to 400°F and line a baking sheet with parchment paper or aluminum foil.
2. Wash the grape tomatoes and cut each in half.
3. Drizzle the olive oil over the tomatoes and season with half a teaspoon each of salt and black pepper. Toss to mix.
4. Spread the tomatoes out on the baking sheet and place in the oven. Cook for 10-12 minutes. Remove from the oven and allow to cool slightly.
5. Place the tomatoes in a bowl and combine them with the chicken, fresh mozzarella, and basil. Drizzle the salad with the balsamic vinegar and season with the remaining salt and black pepper. Toss gently.
6. Serve immediately, or cover and refrigerate for 30 minutes before serving.

Nutritional Information:
Calories 276, Total Fat 14.1 g, Saturated Fat 5.5 g, Total Carbohydrate 3.5 g, Dietary Fiber 0.0 g, Sugars 1.5 g, Protein 30.7 g

4PTS PUMPKIN TASTE SOUP RECIPE

Prep time: 6 minutes
Cooking time: 10 minutes
Servings: 3
Ingredients:
- Olive oil – 2 tbsp.
- Onion (chopped) – 1
- Carrots (chopped) – 1
- Garlic (minced) – 2 cloves
- Curry powder – 2 tsp.
- Salt to taste
- Vegetable broth – 4 cups
- Pumpkin seeds – 2 tbsp.
- Parsley to garnish

Directions:
1. Add oil in the instant pot and let it sauté.
2. Add vegetable broth, pumpkin seeds, salt, curry powder, garlic, carrots and onion in it.
3. Let it cook on high pressure for 10 minutes.
4. When done, serve!

Nutrition:
- Calories: 100g
- Fat: 10g
- Carbohydrates: 8g
- Protein: 110g

6PTS TURKEY MIXED SOUP RECIPE

Prep time: 5 minutes
Cooking time: 15 minutes
Servings: 2
Ingredients:
- Turkey (cubes) – 3 cups
- Water – 2 cups
- Celery – 3 stalks chopped
- Garlic cloves – 2
- Onion (chopped) – 2
- Salt and pepper to taste
- Green onion (chopped) – 2 cups

Directions:
1. Add water and turkey cubes to the instant pot.
2. Add celery, garlic, salt and pepper, onion and green onion in it. Stir well.
3. Cook it on high pressure for 15 minutes. When ready, serve!

Nutrition:
- Calories: 155
- Fat: 7g
- Carbohydrates: 10g
- Protein: 40g

3PTS MUSHROOMS SOUP RECIPE

Prep time: 6 minutes
Cooking time: 10 minutes
Servings: 3
Ingredients:
- Butter – 2 tbsp.
- Onion (chopped) – 1
- Salt to taste
- Mushrooms (chopped) – 3 cups
- Garlic cloves – 2
- Thyme (chopped) – 2 cups
- Flour – 2 tbsp.
- Chicken stock – 3 cups
- Parmesan cheese (shredded) – 2 cups

Directions:
1. Add butter and onion in the instant pot. Add mushrooms, garlic cloves, thyme, chicken stock and flour in it. Mix salt.
2. Let it cook on high pressure for 10 minutes. When done, sprinkle shredded cheese on it and enjoy!

Nutrition:
- Calories: 90
- Fat: 8g
- Carbohydrates: 20g
- Protein: 25g

4PTS SIMPLE CHICKEN AND GREEN ONION SOUP

Prep time: 4 minutes
Cooking time: 10 minutes
Servings: 3
Ingredients:
- Chicken breast (shredded) – 1 lb.
- Chicken stock – 2 cups
- Ginger – 1 tbsp.
- Sesame oil – 2 tbsp.
- Salt to taste
- Green onions (chopped) – 3

Directions:
1. Add sesame oil in the instant pot and let it sauté.
2. Add chicken stock, chicken breast, ginger, salt and green onions
3. Cook on high pressure for 10 minutes.
4. When ready, serve!

Nutrition:
- Calories:10g
- Fat: 6g
- Carbohydrates: 10g
- Protein: 200g

5PTS Instant Pot Egg Salad

Serves: 4, 5 Smart Points™

Ingredients:
- 4 large eggs
- 2 large egg whites
- 2 tablespoon mayonnaise (reduced-calorie)
- 1 teaspoon fresh dill, shopped
- 2 tablespoon fresh chives, chopped
- 1/2 teaspoon Dijon mustard
- ½ teaspoon table salt or to taste
- ¼ teaspoon black pepper, freshly ground

Directions:
1. Place all 6 eggs in a saucepan and add water to cover.
2. Cover the saucepan with a lid and set it over high heat to boil. Boil for about 10 minutes, and drain the water.

3. Place the eggs in ice water to cool so you'll be able to handle them. When the eggs are cool, remove and discard the shells from all the 6 eggs and the yolks of 2 eggs, keeping the egg whites.
4. Cut the 4 whole eggs and the 2 egg whites into ½-inch pieces with a knife or an egg slicer.
5. Transfer the cut eggs to a medium bowl and add the mayonnaise, dill, chives, mustard, salt and pepper.
6. Mix all the ingredients together until they have blended well.
7. Serve and enjoy.

Nutritional Information:
Calories 106, Total Fat 7.3 g, Saturated Fat 1.9 g, Total Carbohydrate 1.3 g, Dietary Fiber 0.1 g, Sugars 1.0 g, Protein 8.2 g

4PTS Spinach, Pears and Blue Cheese Tossed Salad

Serves: 4, 4 Smart Points™

Ingredients:
- 4 tablespoons balsamic vinegar
- 4 teaspoons maple syrup
- Salt to taste
- 2 tablespoons olive oil
- 6 cups mixed baby spinach leaves
- 2 medium pears, sliced
- ¼ cup blue cheese, chopped
- 1 tablespoon pine nuts (optional)

Directions:
1. Mix the vinegar, maple syrup, salt, and olive oil in a small bowl. Mix well until everything has combined properly.
2. Mix the baby spinach, lettuce, and pears in a large bowl and sprinkle the salad with the dressing. Toss to coat.
3. Spread the blue cheese and the pine nuts on top of the salad. Serve immediately.

Nutritional Information:
Calories 149, Total Fat 9.7 g, Saturated Fat 2.6 g, Total Carbohydrate 15.0 g, Dietary Fiber 3.6 g, Sugars 7.0 g, Protein 3.4 g

8PTS Delicious Sweet Potato Chili

Serves: 4, 8 Smart Points™

Ingredients:
- 2 teaspoons olive oil
- 1 cup red onion, diced
- 4 cups sweet potatoes, peeled and cut into small cubes
- 1 teaspoon salt
- 1 teaspoon coarse ground black pepper

- 1 tablespoon chili powder
- ½ teaspoon cinnamon
- 2 cups black beans, cooked or canned
- 4 cups vegetable stock
- 2 cups fresh or jarred salsa
- Fresh cilantro for garnish (optional)

Directions:
1. Place the olive oil in a large saucepan or stock pot over medium heat.
2. Add the onions and sauté for 3 minutes.
3. Add the sweet potatoes, salt, black pepper, chili powder and cinnamon. Cook, stirring frequently, for 3 minutes.
4. Next add the remaining ingredients including the black beans, vegetable stock, and salsa. Mix well.
5. Increase the heat to medium high and cook until the liquid begins to boil. Cover and reduce the heat to low. Simmer for 20 minutes, or until the sweet potatoes are tender.
6. Serve warm, garnished with fresh cilantro, if desired.

Nutritional Information:
Calories 324, Total Fat 3.7 g, Saturated Fat 0.6 g, Total Carbohydrate 71.1 g, Dietary Fiber 16.3 g, Sugars 2.5 g, Protein 15.7 g

6PTS Roasted Cauliflower and Fennel Soup

Serves: 6, 6 Smart Points™

Ingredients:
8 cups cauliflower florets (approximately one large head)
1 cup yellow onion, sliced
1 cup fennel bulb, sliced
2 tablespoons olive oil
2 teaspoons fresh rosemary, chopped
½ teaspoon nutmeg
1 teaspoon salt
1 teaspoon black pepper
6 cups vegetable stock
½ cup pancetta, diced

Directions:
1. Preheat the oven to 450°F and line a baking sheet with aluminum foil.
2. In a bowl, toss together the cauliflower, onion, and fennel. Drizzle the vegetables with olive oil and season with rosemary, nutmeg, salt, and black pepper. Toss to mix.
3. Spread the vegetables out on a baking sheet and place them in the oven. Bake for 15 minutes.
4. While the vegetables are roasting, bring the vegetable stock to a boil in a soup pot over medium high heat.
5. Place the pancetta in a small skillet over medium heat, and cook for 3-5 minutes, stirring frequently, until lightly crispy.
6. Remove the vegetables from the oven and carefully transfer to the boiling vegetable stock. Cover, reduce the heat to low and simmer for 10-14 minutes.

7. Working in batches, transfer the soup to a blender or food processor and puree before adding the soup back to the pot. Continue with the remaining soup until the desired consistency has been reached.
8. Serve warm, garnished with crispy pancetta.

Nutritional Information:
Calories 196, Total Fat 8.2 g, Saturated Fat 2.0 g, Total Carbohydrate 25.8 g, Dietary Fiber 9.4 g, Sugars 3.8 g, Protein 8.9 g

5PTS Quick French Onion Soup

Serves: 6, 5 Smart Points™

Ingredients:
- Cooking spray, preferably butter flavored
- 2 large sweet onions, sliced
- 2 large red onions, sliced
- 1 bay leaf
- 4 garlic cloves, minced
- 1 teaspoon fresh thyme, chopped
- ½ cup red wine
- 1 tablespoon Worcestershire sauce
- 1 tablespoon balsamic vinegar
- 1 teaspoon salt
- ½ teaspoon pepper, freshly ground
- 6 cups fat free beef broth
- ¼ cup fresh chives, or scallions, minced
- 6 slices whole wheat bread, light
- 1 cup cheese (preferably Fontina), shredded

Directions:
1. Spray a large saucepan with nonfat cooking spray, preferably butter flavored, and place it over medium-high heat.
2. Add the sliced sweet onions and red onions. Toss them lightly and cover. Reduce the heat to medium and cook until soft. Stir regularly until the mixture starts to brown, which should take about 6-8 minutes.
3. Add the bay leaf, garlic, and thyme, and continue cooking, uncovered. Stir regularly, about 3-4 minutes.
3. Pour in the red wine, Worcestershire sauce, vinegar, salt, and pepper and stir thoroughly. Increase the heat to medium-high and bring the mixture to simmer. Let it continue cooking, and stir until most of the liquid has evaporated, about 1-2 minutes.
4. Mix in the broth, stir and let it boil. Reduce the heat to simmer and cook for another 3 minutes.
5. Remove from the heat and add the minced fresh chives or scallions.
6. In the meantime, toast the 6 slices of bread and place them in bowls. Top them with the shredded cheese. Spoon the soup over the cheese and bread and serve.

Nutritional Information:
Calories 138, Total Fat 6.0 g, Total Carbohydrate 18.0 g, Dietary Fiber 4.0 g, Protein 15.0 g

5PTS Oyster Mushroom Egg Drop Soup

Serves: 4, 5 Smart Points™

Ingredients:
4 cups chicken stock
5 wonton wrappers

1 cup oyster mushrooms, thinly sliced
2 eggs, beaten
1 teaspoon soy sauce
½ teaspoon salt
1 teaspoon white pepper
Scallions, sliced for garnish (optional)
Lime slices for garnish (optional)

Directions:
1. Place the chicken stock in a soup pan and bring it to a boil over medium-high heat. Once the stock comes to a boil, reduce the heat to medium low.
2. While the stock is coming to a boil, lay the wonton wrappers out on the counter and slice them into ½-inch thick pieces.
3. Add the mushrooms and sliced wonton wrappers to the chicken stock and cook for 1-2 minutes.
4. In a bowl, combine the beaten eggs, soy sauce, salt, and white pepper. Whisk together.
5. Slowly pour the egg mixture into the soup, whisking constantly to create thin strips of cooked egg throughout the soup. Cook for an additional 1-2 minutes.
6. Remove the soup from the heat and serve warm, garnished with scallions and lime, if desired.

Nutritional Information:
Calories 151, Total Fat 5.3 g, Saturated Fat 1.6 g, Total Carbohydrate 15.1 g, Dietary Fiber 0.5 g, Sugars 3.9 g, Protein 10.4 g

3PTS Chicken and Egg Soup

Serves: 4

3 Smart Points™

Ingredients:

4 cups chicken broth (low sodium)

½ teaspoon soy sauce

½ cup boneless skinless chicken breast, cooked and chopped

½ cup frozen green baby peas

¼ cup green onion, thinly sliced

1 egg, lightly beaten

Directions:
1. Put the chicken stock and soy sauce in a saucepan and bring it to a boil. Add the cooked chicken, baby peas and sliced green onion and let it boil again.

2. Remove the pot from the heat and add the egg as you stir steadily. Allow the soup to sit for 1 minute so the egg can set.
3. Stir gently and serve in bowls.

Nutritional Information:

Calories 119, Total Fat 4.0 g, Saturated Fat 1.0 g, Total Carbohydrate 8.0 g, Dietary Fiber 2.0 g, Sugars 2.5 g, Protein 14.0 g

VEGETARIAN RECIPES

4PTS ZUCCHINI SOBA NOODLES

Serves: 4, 4 Smart Points™

Ingredients:

2 cups zucchini, julienned

½ pound soba noodles, cooked

2 teaspoons sesame oil

½ cup rice vinegar

1 tablespoon soy sauce

1 tablespoon honey

½ teaspoon salt

1 teaspoon black pepper

1 teaspoon crushed red pepper flakes

¼ cup fresh parsley, chopped (optional)

Directions:

1. Place 4 cups of water in a saucepan and bring it to a boil. Add the zucchini to the water and cook for 2 minutes.
2. Using a skimmer or colander, remove the zucchini from the water and immediately rinse with cold water to stop the cooking. Drain well.
3. Place the cooked soba noodles in a bowl and drizzle with the sesame oil. Toss to coat.
4. In a separate bowl, combine the rice vinegar, soy sauce, and honey. Whisk until well blended.
5. Add the drained zucchini to the noodles and pour the rice vinegar dressing over the top. Toss to coat.
6. Season with salt, black pepper, crushed red pepper flakes, and fresh parsley, if using. Toss gently once again.
7. Serve immediately or chill for several hours before serving as a cold salad.

Nutritional Information:

Calories 135, Total Fat 2.4 g, Saturated Fat 0.3 g, Total Carbohydrate 26.2 g, Dietary Fiber 1.3 g, Sugars 5.8 g, Protein 4.9 g

5PTS PERFECT GARDEN PASTA

Serves: 4
5 Smart Points™

Ingredients:
2 tablespoons olive oil or vegetable spray
1 ½ cups asparagus, cut into 1-inch pieces
1 cup fresh snow peas, trimmed
1 ½ cups Roma tomatoes, chopped
1 pound whole wheat pasta shells, cooked
¼ cup fresh basil, chopped
1 teaspoon salt
1 teaspoon black pepper
½ teaspoon garlic powder

Directions:
1. Place the olive oil or cooking spray in a large skillet over medium heat.
2. Add the asparagus and snow peas. Cook, stirring frequently, until just tender, approximately 5 minutes.
3. Add the Roma tomatoes and cook an additional 2-3 minutes, slightly breaking up the tomatoes with a wooden spoon to release their juices.
4. Add the pasta and basil to the skillet. Season with salt, black pepper, and garlic powder. Toss to mix.
5. Cook until heated through and the flavors are blended, approximately 2-3 additional minutes.
6. Remove from the heat and serve immediately.

Nutritional Information:
Calories 201, Total Fat 1.1 g, Saturated Fat 0.2 g, Total Carbohydrate 42.8 g, Dietary Fiber 8.4 g, Sugars 0.8 g, Protein 9.5 g

7PTS CHICKPEA AND SPINACH FRITTATA

Serves: 4, 7 Smart Points™

Ingredients:

Cooking spray

2 cloves garlic, crushed and minced

4 cups fresh spinach, torn

8 eggs

¼ cup freshly grated Parmesan cheese

1 teaspoon salt

1 teaspoon black pepper

2 teaspoons fresh rosemary, finely chopped

1 cup chickpeas, canned or cooked

Directions:

1. Preheat the oven to 400°F and line a spring form pan with parchment paper. Spray the sides of the spring form pan with cooking spray.
2. Prepare a skillet with cooking spray and heat over medium.
3. Add the garlic and sauté for 1-2 minutes before adding the spinach. Continue to cook for 2-3 minutes, or until the spinach is wilted. Remove from heat and set aside.
4. In a bowl, combine the eggs, Parmesan, salt, black pepper, and rosemary. Using a whisk, blend well until the eggs are yellow and creamy.
5. Place the chickpeas in the spring form pan, and arrange the spinach on them in a layer.
6. Pour the egg mixture into the pan and tap gently to even it out.
7. Place the pan on a baking sheet, and in the oven.
8. Bake for 20-25 minutes, or until it is golden on top and the middle of the frittata is springy to the touch.

Nutritional Information:

Calories 239, Total Fat 11.5 g, Saturated Fat 4.0 g, Total Carbohydrate 15.6 g, Dietary Fiber 3.3 g, Sugars 0.5 g, Protein 18.0 g

7PTS MEDITERRANEAN STUFFED SWEET POTATOES

Serves: 4, 7 Smart Points™

Ingredients:

- 4 medium-sized sweet potatoes
- ¼ cup hummus
- Cooking spray
- 4 cups fresh spinach
- 1 cup tomatoes, diced
- 1 teaspoon salt
- 1 teaspoon black pepper
- ½ teaspoon onion powder
- 1 teaspoon crushed red pepper flakes
- ½ cup feta cheese

Directions:

1. Wash and dry each of the sweet potatoes and pierce the skins in several places using a fork.
2. Place the sweet potatoes in the microwave and cook until completely tender on the inside, approximately 5-7 minutes, depending on the size of the potato. Remove them from the microwave and let them cool just enough to comfortably handle.
3. Slice the sweet potatoes in half and scoop out the insides. Transfer the insides to a bowl and combine with the hummus. Mix well and set aside.
4. Prepare a skillet using the cooking spray and heat it over medium.
5. Add the spinach and tomatoes. Cook for 2-3 minutes, or until the spinach is wilted.
6. Add the sweet potato mixture to the skillet, and then season it with salt, black pepper, onion powder, and crushed red pepper flakes. Mix well.
7. Transfer the sweet potato mixture back into the sweet potato shells.
8. Garnish with feta cheese immediately before serving.

Nutritional Information:

Calories 220, Total Fat 5.7 g, Saturated Fat 3.1 g, Total Carbohydrate 37.0 g, Dietary Fiber 5.7 g, Sugars 0.1 g, Protein 6.9 g

8PTS EGGPLANT AND COUSCOUS RAGU

Serves: 4
8 Smart Points™

Ingredients:
1 tablespoon olive oil
4 cups eggplant, peeled and cubed
1 cup onion, chopped
4 cloves garlic, crushed and minced
4 cups stewed tomatoes, including liquid, chopped
1 teaspoon salt
1 teaspoon black pepper
4 cups couscous, cooked
¼ cup fresh basil, chopped (optional)
¼ fresh grated Parmesan (optional)

Directions:
1. Heat the olive oil in a large skillet over medium.
2. Add the eggplant and onion. Sauté for 5-7 minutes.
3. Next, add the garlic and tomatoes. Season with salt and black pepper. Cook for an additional 3-4 minutes, stirring frequently.
4. Reduce the heat and let the mixture simmer for 3 minutes.
5. Spoon the cooked couscous into serving dishes and top with the eggplant ragu.
6. Garnish with fresh basil and Parmesan, if desired, before serving.

Nutritional Information:
Calories 281, Total Fat 4.4 g, Saturated Fat 0.6 g, Total Carbohydrate 53.2 g, Dietary Fiber 6.9 g, Sugars 0.0 g, Protein 8.8 g

5PTS VEGETARIAN PITA PIZZA

Serves: 1, 5 Smart Points™

Ingredients:
- 1 large pita bread, thin
- ¼ cup pizza sauce
- ¼ cup green pepper
- ¼ cup mushrooms
- 10 small black olives
- ½ cup mozzarella cheese
- 2 teaspoons Parmesan cheese
- 1 pinch pizza seasoning or oregano

Directions:
1. Place the pita bread on a flat surface and spread the pizza sauce on top.
2. Arrange the vegetables over the sauce, as well as the mozzarella cheese. Top this with the Parmesan cheese and the seasoning.
3. Spray the cooking spray over the cheese, but do it lightly.
4. Set oven on the broil mode. Place the pizza in the oven for about 2 minutes or until the cheese is melted and golden.
5. Remove from the oven and serve.

Nutritional Information:
Calories 341, Total Fat 5.9 g, Saturated Fat 1.4 g, Total Carbohydrate 45.3 g, Dietary Fiber 5.4 g, Sugars 4.0 g, Protein 27.2 g

3PTS CORN TOMATO SALAD

Serves: 6, 3 Smart Points™

Ingredients:
6 ears of corn, husks and silk removed
¾ cup cherry tomatoes, halved
½ cup green onions, thinly sliced
2 tablespoons extra-virgin olive oil
2 tablespoons fresh lime juice, or cider vinegar
Salt and pepper to taste

Directions:
1. Cut the corn kernels from the cobs into a large bowl. Add all the other ingredients and combine well. Cover the bowl and let it to sit for 15 minutes so the flavors can mingle. Serve.

Nutritional Information:
Calories 110, Total Fat 5.4 g, Saturated Fat 1.0 g, Total Carbohydrate 15.7 g, Dietary Fiber 2.4 g, Sugars 3.1 g, Protein 2.7 g

5PTS CAULIFLOWER AND BLACK BEANS

Serves: 4, 5 Smart Points™

Ingredients:

1 medium-sized cauliflower
Cooking spray (non-fat) or olive oil spray
1 cup black beans, drained and rinsed
1 medium-sized tomato, diced
1 teaspoon cumin
1 teaspoon garlic powder
Salt and pepper to taste
1 cup sharp cheddar cheese (reduced fat), shredded
4 slices lean turkey bacon, diced and cooked
4 scallions, diced
½ cup sour cream (fat free)

Directions:

1. Prepare the cauliflower into bite-sized florets and steam them in a pot, or in the microwave in a lidded bowl with an inch of water.
2. When the cauliflower is tender, coat a small, nonstick skillet with cooking spray and set it over medium high heat. Add the drained black beans, diced tomato, cumin, and garlic powder. Sauté for about 2 minutes, or until the mixture has been heated through. Remove from the heat and divide it into 4 portions.
3. Place the cooked cauliflower on 4 serving bowls and then season with salt and pepper to taste.
4. Divide the cheese into 4 parts and top each serving with a portion. Microwave 1 minute each, or wait until the cheese has melted. Remove from the microwave and top each serving with the black beans and tomato mixture.
5. Top each with 2 tablespoons of fat-free sour cream, cooked bacon, and scallions. Serve and enjoy.

Nutritional Information:

Calories 253, Total Fat 6.5 g, Saturated Fat 1.3 g, Total Carbohydrate 29.0 g, Dietary Fiber 10.0 g, Sugars 12.4 g, Protein 13.0 g

5PTS ZUCCHINI CASHEW NOODLES

Serves: 4
5 Smart Points™

Ingredients:
6 cups zucchini, spiral cut into noodles
¼ cup cashew butter
¼ cup ponzu or soy sauce
1 tablespoon chili garlic paste
1 tablespoon freshly grated ginger
1 tablespoon olive oil
½ teaspoon salt
1 teaspoon black pepper
1 teaspoon five spice powder
Fresh scallions for garnish, if desired

Directions:
1. In a bowl, combine the cashew butter, ponzu or soy sauce, chili garlic paste and freshly grated ginger. Whisk until well blended and set aside.
2. Heat the olive oil in a skillet over medium heat.
3. Add the zucchini and season with salt, black pepper, and five spice powder.
4. Cook for 5-7 minutes, stirring frequently, until the zucchini is firm tender.
5. Pour the sauce over the zucchini, toss and cook for an additional 1-2 minutes, or until heated through.
6. Serve warm, garnished with fresh scallions, if desired.

Nutritional Information:
Calories 149, Total Fat 9.4 g, Saturated Fat 1.7 g, Total Carbohydrate 13.9 g, Dietary Fiber 4.1 g, Sugars 5.7 g, Protein 4.0 g

SIDE DISHES AND SNACKS

2PTS SESAME ASPARAGUS

Serves: 4, 2 Smart Points™

Ingredients:

1 pound asparagus spears
2 tablespoons rice vinegar
1 teaspoon sesame oil
1 tablespoon shallots, diced
½ teaspoon salt
1 teaspoon black pepper
1 tablespoon sesame seeds

Directions:

1. Preheat the oven to 450°F and line a baking sheet with aluminum foil or parchment paper.
2. Wash, trim and cut the asparagus spears in half.
3. In a bowl, combine the rice vinegar, sesame oil, and shallots. Whisk them together, and then pour over the asparagus spears. Toss to coat.
4. Spread the asparagus out on the baking sheet and season with salt and pepper.
5. Bake for 15 minutes.
6. Remove from the oven and garnish with sesame seeds before serving.

Nutritional Information:

Calories 49, Total Fat 2.4 g, Saturated Fat 0.3 g, Total Carbohydrate 6.4 g, Dietary Fiber 1.6 g, Sugars 2.5 g, Protein 1.9 g

2PTS HERBED GREEN BEANS

Serves 4, 2 Smart Points™

Ingredients

4 cups green beans, trimmed
1 tablespoon olive oil
2 cloves garlic, crushed and minced
½ cup fresh mint, chopped

½ cup fresh parsley, chopped
1 teaspoon lemon zest
1 teaspoon coarse ground black pepper

Directions

1. Heat the olive oil in a large sauté pan over medium heat. Add the green beans and garlic.
2. Sauté until the green beans are crisp tender, approximately 5-6 minutes.
3. Add the mint, parsley, lemon zest, and black pepper. Toss to coat.
4. Serve immediately.

Nutritional Information:

Calories 66, Total Fat 3.5 g, Saturated Fat 0.5 g, Total Carbohydrate 8.3 g, Dietary Fiber 3.8 g, Sugars 0 g, Protein 2.1 g

3PTS FRESH SPINACH MUFFINS

Serves 18, 3 Smart Points™

Ingredients

1 tablespoon olive oil
1 cup red onion, diced
1 cup fresh spinach, torn
½ cup low sodium bacon, cooked and crumbled
2 teaspoons crushed red pepper flakes

1 ¼ cup whole wheat flour
2 teaspoons baking powder
2 eggs, beaten
1 ½ cup low fat milk
1 cup feta cheese, crumbled
½ cup fresh grated Parmesan cheese

Directions

1. Preheat oven to 325°F and lightly oil 18 muffin tins.
2. Add the olive oil to a sauté pan and heat over medium. Add the onion and sauté for 2-3 minutes. Add the spinach, bacon, and crushed red pepper. Sauté until spinach is wilted, approximately 1 minute.
3. In a bowl, combine the wheat flour and baking soda.
4. In another bowl combine the eggs, milk, feta cheese and Parmesan cheese.
5. Incorporate the dry ingredients into the wet and then fold in the spinach.
6. Spoon the mixture into muffin tins.
7. Place the muffin tins into the oven and bake for 35 minutes or until golden.
8. Let cool before serving.

Nutritional Information:

Calories 92, Total Fat 4.4 g, Saturated Fat 2.2 g, Total Carbohydrate 8.6 g, Dietary Fiber 1.2 g, Sugars 1.1 g, Protein 5.2 g

3PTS CRISP FENNEL AND PEAR

Serves 2, 3 Smart Points™

Ingredients:

1 cup fennel, thinly sliced

2 cups pear, thinly sliced

¼ cup champagne vinegar

¼ cup fresh mint, chopped

½ teaspoon black pepper

Directions:

1. Combine the fennel and pear in a bowl.
2. In another bowl, combine the champagne vinegar, mint, and black pepper. Whisk well.
3. Pour the dressing over the salad and toss to coat.
4. Refrigerate at least 2 hours before serving.

Nutritional Information:

Calories 119, Total Fat 0.4 g, Saturated Fat 0 g, Total Carbohydrate 29.3 g, Dietary Fiber 7.3 g, Sugars 15.8 g, Protein 1.6 g

3PTS SHAVED BRUSSELS SPROUTS WITH WALNUTS

Serves 4, 3 Smart Points™

Ingredients:

4 cups Brussels sprouts, shaved
2 tablespoons olive oil
½ cup red onion, diced
1 teaspoon thyme
1 teaspoon black pepper
¼ cup walnuts, chopped
¼ cup fresh shaved Parmesan

Directions:

1. Heat the olive oil in a skillet over medium heat. Add the onions and sauté until tender, approximately 2-3 minutes.
2. Add the Brussels sprouts and cook for 5 minutes. Season with thyme and black pepper.
3. Remove from heat and stir in the walnuts.
4. Garnish with fresh Parmesan for serving.

Nutritional Information:

Calories 103, Total Fat 6.4 g, Saturated Fat 1.4 g, Total Carbohydrate 8.8 g, Dietary Fiber 3.2 g, Sugars 2.0 g, Protein 2.7 g

2PTS CREAMY CARROT SLAW

Serves: 4
2 Smart Points™

Ingredients:
2 cups carrots, shredded
1 cup celery, chopped
1 cup tart apple, diced
¼ cup low fat mayonnaise
1 tablespoon apple cider vinegar
1 teaspoon salt
1 teaspoon black pepper
Fresh scallions for garnish (optional)

Directions:
1. Combine the carrots, celery, and apple in a bowl. Toss to mix.
2. In a separate bowl, combine the low fat mayonnaise, apple cider vinegar, salt, and black pepper. Whisk until well blended.
3. Add the dressing to the salad and toss gently until mixed together.
4. Cover and refrigerate for at least 20 minutes before serving.
5. Garnish with fresh scallions, if desired.

Nutritional Information:
Calories 55, Total Fat 0.9 g, Saturated Fat 0.0 g, Total Carbohydrate 12.1 g, Dietary Fiber 2.8 g, Sugars 5.8 g, Protein 0.8 g

3PTS DECADENT MUSHROOMS

Serves: 4
3 Smart Points™

Ingredients:
2 cups assorted mushrooms, sliced
2 cloves garlic, crushed and minced
Cooking spray
½ cup fat free cream cheese
¼ cup crème fraiche
1 tablespoon fresh chives, chopped
1 teaspoon salt
1 teaspoon black pepper
½ teaspoon thyme

Directions:
1. Prepare a skillet with the cooking spray and heat over medium.
2. Add the mushrooms and garlic to the skillet and sauté for 3-4 minutes.
3. Add the cream cheese, crème fraiche, and fresh chives.
4. Season with salt, black pepper, and thyme. Cook, stirring frequently, to blend the cream cheese and crème fraiche, for 3 minutes.
5. Remove from heat and serve immediately.

Nutritional Information:
Calories 79, Total Fat 4.2 g, Saturated Fat 2.6 g, Total Carbohydrate 3.5 g, Dietary Fiber 0.4 g, Sugars 2.0 g, Protein 5.5 g

5PTS LEMON WALNUT QUINOA

Serves: 6
5 Smart Points™

Ingredients:
2 cups chicken stock
1 cup quinoa
¼ cup walnuts, chopped
2 teaspoons lemon zest
1 teaspoon salt
1 teaspoon black pepper
1 teaspoon tarragon
¼ cup goat cheese

Directions:
1. Pour the chicken stock in a saucepan over medium-high heat and bring it to a boil.
2. Stir in the quinoa, reduce the heat to low, cover, and simmer for 15-20 minutes or until tender.
3. Remove the quinoa from the heat and fluff it with a fork.
4. Stir in the walnuts, lemon zest, salt, black pepper, and tarragon. Mix well.
5. Transfer the quinoa to serving dishes and garnish with bits of goat cheese before serving.

Nutritional Information:
Calories 193, Total Fat 7.6 g, Saturated Fat 1.5 g, Total Carbohydrate 24.3 g, Dietary Fiber 2.3 g, Sugars 3.5 g, Protein 7.8 g

2PTS SPICED BRUSSELS SPROUTS

Serves: 4
2 Smart Points™

Ingredients:
4 cups Brussels sprouts, halved
1 cup onion, sliced
1 tablespoon olive oil
1 teaspoon cinnamon
½ teaspoon cayenne powder
1 teaspoon salt
1 teaspoon black pepper

Directions:
1. Preheat the oven to 450°F and line a baking sheet with aluminum foil.
2. Place the Brussels sprouts and onions in a bowl.
3. Drizzle the vegetables with olive oil and then season with the cinnamon, cayenne powder, salt and black pepper. Toss to coat.
4. Spread the vegetables out onto the baking sheet.
5. Place in the oven and roast for 20-25 minutes, tossing occasionally.
6. Remove from the oven and let cool slightly before serving.

Nutritional Information:
Calories 79, Total Fat 3.7 g, Saturated Fat 0.5 g, Total Carbohydrate 10.4 g, Dietary Fiber 3.9 g, Sugars 1.9 g, Protein 3.3 g

DESSERTS RECIPES

2PTS TASTY CUPCAKE BROWNIES

Serves: 12, 2 Smart Points™

Ingredients:

¾ cup all-purpose flour

½ cup sugar, preferably brown

3 tablespoons cocoa, unsweetened

½ teaspoon baking soda

¼ teaspoon salt

½ cup water

¼ cup applesauce, unsweetened

1 tablespoon brown sugar, firmly packed

1 ½ teaspoons margarine, melted

½ teaspoon vanilla extract

½ teaspoon cider vinegar

Cooking spray (optional)

Directions:
1. Preheat the oven to 350°F.
2. In a large bowl, combine the flour, brown sugar, unsweetened cocoa, baking soda, and salt. Mix well.
3. In another bowl, stir together all the other ingredients. Pour the mixture over the flour mixture and stir just until the batter is smooth.
3. Coat a nonstick muffin tin with 12 cups with vegetable oil spray, or line them with paper liners. Pour the batter into the muffin cups until they're half full.
4. Bake for 18 to 20 minutes. To ensure that the cupcakes are cooked, prick them in the center with a toothpick and if it comes out clean, they are ready. Remove them from the oven and let them stand for 5 minutes before transferring them to the rack to cool. Enjoy.

Nutritional Information:

Calories 78, Total Fat 0.7 g, Saturated Fat 0.2 g, Total Carbohydrate 17.3 g, Dietary Fiber 0.7 g, Sugars 10.6 g, Protein 1.1 g

5PTS QUICK BANANA ROLL UPS

Serves: 1, 5 Smart Points™

Ingredients:
1 6-inch whole wheat tortilla
1 tablespoon peanut butter (reduced-fat)
1 teaspoon raspberry jam (sugar-free)
1 teaspoon dried coconut (unsweetened), shredded
½ medium-sized ripe banana, sliced

Directions:
1. Lay the whole wheat tortilla on a flat surface and spread the peanut butter and jam evenly on it. Sprinkle the dried shredded coconut on top.
2. Arrange the banana pieces on the tortilla. Roll up the tortilla to enclose the banana pieces. Wrap it in a paper towel and put in the microwave on high mode for 30 to 35 seconds.
3. Remove from microwave and unwrap from the paper towel. Enjoy.

Nutritional Information:
Calories 160, Total Fat 7.0 g, Saturated Fat 1.0 g, Total Carbohydrate 25.0 g, Dietary Fiber 3.0 g, Sugars 12.0 g, Protein 5.0 g

4PTS FRUIT AND PUDDING MIX DESSERT

Serves: 6, 4 Smart Points™

Ingredients:
1 (20 ounce) can pineapple chunks
1 (15 ounce) can oranges
1 (5 ⅛ ounces) vanilla pudding mix (sugar-free and low-fat), preferably instant

Directions:
1. Drain the fruit juices into a bowl and add the dry pudding. This will help to mix the pudding so you don't have to add milk.
2. Add all the other ingredients and blend them well. Chill the dessert. Serve and enjoy.

Nutritional Information:
Calories 94, Total Fat 0.3 g, Saturated Fat 0.0 g, Total Carbohydrate 24.3 g, Dietary Fiber 2.0 g, Sugars 21.1 g, Protein 1.0 g

1PTS BANANA "ICE CREAM" DESSERT

Serves: 2, 1 Smart Points™

Ingredients:

2 ripe bananas, peeled

2 tablespoons skim milk or fruit juice

1 teaspoon vanilla extract

Directions:

1. Cut the banana into chunks and freeze them. Put the frozen banana chunks in a blender or food processor and puree.
2. Add the vanilla extract and milk or juice to make soft banana "ice cream" dessert. Serve the same way you serve ice cream and layer with strawberries. You may add other frozen fruits of your choice such as mango or pineapple. You can also serve it with chocolate syrup.

Nutritional Information:

Calories 121, Total Fat 0.9 g, Saturated Fat.0 g

Total Carbohydrate 27.9 g, Dietary Fiber 3.1 g, Sugars 14.7 g, Protein 1.8 g

0PTS NO POINT BANANA STRAWBERRY "ICE CREAM" DESSERT

Serves: 1, 0 Smart Points™

Ingredients:

1 ripe bananas, peeled

3 fresh strawberries for serving, sliced

Directions:

1. Cut the banana into chunks and freeze them. Put the frozen banana chunks in a blender or food processor and puree.
2. Serve ice cream with sliced strawberries. You may add other fruits of your choice such as mango or pineapple.

Nutritional Information:

Calories 127.8, Total Fat 1.1 g, Saturated Fat 0 g, Total Carbohydrate 32.7 g, Dietary Fiber 4.3 g, Sugars 17.7 g, Protein 2.1 g

1PTS SIMPLE FROZEN FRUIT DESSERT

Serves: 24, 1 Smart Points™

Ingredients:

1 can whole berry cranberry sauce
1 can pineapple, crushed
1 container whipped topping (fat free)
1/4 cup walnuts, chopped

Directions:

1. Mix all the ingredients together and combine well. Divide the mixture into 24 cupcake pans with liners. Freeze. Remove the frozen desserts and place them in a plastic bag and then store in the freezer. Enjoy one whenever you want something sweet and cold.

Nutritional Information:

Calories 63, Total Fat 0.8 g, Saturated Fat 0.2 g Total Carbohydrate 13.4 g, Dietary Fiber 0.6 g, Sugars 9.1g, Protein 0.1 g

2PTS COCONUT AND CRANBERRY MACAROONS

Serves: 12, 2 macaroons per serving
2 Smart Points™

Ingredients:
2 egg whites (large size)
¼ teaspoon salt
⅓ Cup sugar
1 cup sweetened flaked coconut
½ cup dried cranberries
2 tablespoons all-purpose flour
½ teaspoon vanilla extract
Cooking spray

Directions:
1. Preheat the oven to 325°F, and coat 2 cooking sheets with vegetable oil spray, or line them with parchment paper.
2. In a medium bowl, combine the egg whites and salt. Use an electric mixer to beat at low speed for about 1 minute, until the egg whites foam.
3. Gradually add the sugar as you increase the mixer speed for about 5 to 7 minutes.
4. Fold in the remaining ingredients. Drop the batter using a tablespoon onto a cookie sheet. Bake for about 15 minutes or until the macaroons become light golden brown. Remove from the oven and serve.

Nutritional Information:
Calories 68. Total Fat 3.0 g, Saturated Fat 1.2 g Total Carbohydrate 10.0 g, Dietary Fiber 0.0 g, Sugars 9.0 g, Protein 1.0 g

2PTS FROZEN PEANUT BUTTER CUPS

Serves: 12, 2 Smart Points™

Ingredients:
Fat free whipped topping (1 tube or approximately 8 ounces), thawed
6 tablespoons peanut butter (creamy)
4 tablespoons chocolate syrup (sugar-free), preferably Hershey's®

Directions:
1. Mix the whipped topping and peanut butter together.
2. Use a spoon to drop the mixture into 12 lined cupcake tins. Drizzle with chocolate syrup. Freeze, and enjoy.

Nutritional Information:
Calories 32, Total Fat 2.0 g, Saturated Fat 0 g Total Carbohydrate 3.0 g, Dietary Fiber 0 g, Sugars 2.0 g, Protein 1.0 g

2PTS INSTANT POT TRUFFLES

Yields 24, 2 truffles per serving, 2 Smart Points™

Ingredients:

1 cup powdered sugar

½ cup cocoa, unsweetened

½ cup fat-free cream cheese

½ teaspoon vanilla extract

Directions:

1. Prepare a baking sheet with parchment paper, and sprinkle it cocoa powder.
2. Mix all the ingredients with an electric mixer. Use a rounded teaspoon to drop the mixture onto the sheet.
3. Roll the mixture into balls and put in the refrigerator. Enjoy.

Nutritional Information:

Calories 36, Total Fat 0 g, Saturated Fat 0 g Total Carbohydrate 6.8 g, Dietary Fiber 0.6 g, Sugars 5.1 g, Protein 0.8 g

3PTS YUMMY PUMPKIN PUDDING

Serves: 2

3 Smart Points™

Ingredients:

1 ½ cups skim milk

1 (15 ounce) can pure pumpkin

½ box instant vanilla pudding (sugar free and fat free)

1 tablespoon ground allspice

1 tablespoon cinnamon

Add brown sugar to taste

Directions:

1. To make thick pumpkin, combine skim milk and pumpkin in a pan and stir. Add the instant pudding and combine.
2. Add the remaining ingredients and stir. Add more seasonings to taste if desired. Heat and stir occasionally until the soup is warm. Enjoy.

Nutritional Information:

Calories 163, Total Fat 0.9 g, Saturated Fat 0.1 g, Total Carbohydrate 30.8 g, Dietary Fiber 1.7 g, Sugars 17.2 g, Protein 9.5 g

END NOTE

Thank for making it through to the end of *this book*. Let's hope it was informative and able to provide you with all of the tools you need to achieve your weight loss goals.

J Beckam

CPSIA information can be obtained
at www.ICGtesting.com
Printed in the USA
LVHW062157291219
642025LV00020B/929/P